Raising Boys into Men

ManCamp

David G. Hamilton

Raising Boys into Men - ManCamp

ISBN (978-0-9887694-0-3)

Printed in USA by …

Phone: (208) 350-9153

Website: www.raisingboysintomen.com

The most important things that you can teach your son are to feel and recognize the Spirit of God and that Jesus Christ atoned for the sins of the world.

Dedication

To God in Heaven
I love Thee, and I will serve thee all my days.

To My Family
To my parents, thank you for your love and support. To my elder brother, you are a great man! To my sons, Austin, Harker, and Scout, thank you for putting up with me as a dad, I have done my best! I know I failed often, please forgive me for my shortcomings. I pray you will be better dads to your kids, than I have been to you. I pray daily for you and I hope you grow up to be honorable men full of integrity and sound mind. I shout praises to God in Heaven for the blessing you have been in my life. To my wife, thank you for your love, encouragement and support. You are my one true-heart's desire. Every single day you make my life better, and I am truly a "rich man" in every sense of the word.

Table of Contents

www.raisingboysintomen.com

The ManCamp Formula

The ManCamp formula has been constructed by combining a Survivalist Boy Scout approach toward camping, coupled with a spiritual element, in a no-nonsense guide that every father can copy.

$$[(Time \times Fun) + (Challenges \times Nature) + (Relationship\ Bank\ Account\ Deposits + Adventure)] \char`\^ The\ Spirit\ of\ God = ManCamp$$

(If you are a math geek like me, I hope you understood the order of operations and found it humorous)

Some of the sample dialogs may not be natural for you. It is important that you remain natural in all your dealings with your son. My wife came from a family that says, "I love you," often, and I came from a family that didn't say it. In raising my own boys, I have learned the value of speaking the words. So, if you are not the verbal type, this may be an opportunity for you to grow as well. We just need to say the words. We need to say, "I love you, I am proud of you." Words of affirmation are important to our son's self-esteem, it is time for you to say them, learn to say them now!

Frequent pats on the back are also essential. I pat my 4 year old repeatedly, almost like a tickle attack, until he smiles, while I tell him how "good" he is. He is attacked like this at least once a day, and so are my other sons. There are very few nights that I let pass by without holding my boys down and tickle them until they yell as loud as they can, "I AM A GOOD BOY!" I then hold them down another few seconds and tickle them some more and lean down and tell them quietly in their ear, "And don't you ever forget that! I love you, and I am proud of you, you are a very good boy!"

ManCamp in the Beginning

"My father gave me the greatest gift anyone could give another person, he believed in me."
– Jim Valvano, Former N.C. State Basketball Coach

ManCamp began because I knew I needed to spend more quality time with my sons. Every man should set aside 3 days a year to attend a ManCamp with his sons. The most important thing is that you try. Please do not be discouraged if you can't do all, most, or some of the ManCamp I present in this book! There is a lot here, and even if you were able to do ½ of what is in this book, you will be a SuperDad in any boys' books! Please don't feel like you need to "rough it," you can complete the entire ManCamp program locally if you need. You could even just go to a motel 30 miles away and order a pizza. The whole purpose of ManCamp is that you connect with, and teach your son life lessons. Your criteria may differ slightly, but for me, the boys must be potty trained. It is a good incentive to any boy learning, and can be a useful tool for a mother to encourage her learning son. "You need to learn to put your potty in the potty or you can't go on ManCamp," were words often echoed in our home, by my wife. It only helped the process. If we want our boys to develop attributes of trustworthiness, we need to start giving our sons responsibilities that can build their abilities and confidence. We need to believe in them!

Your ManCamp can be as long or as short as you would like it to be. Three days is a good camp, and will have sufficient time to accomplish all that you set out to do. Perhaps your work schedule will only allow one night in the backyard, or perhaps you love to camp and want to be outdoors for many more days. This itinerary is not comprehensive; adjust for your interests and the interests of your son.

Responsibilities as a Father

"The father who does not teach his son his duties is equally guilty with the son who neglects them." – Confucius

5

Fathers stand-up and take responsibility for the rearing of your children. Take an active role. On judgment day, you will stand before God and you will report your stewardship in this life. You will be held accountable for the father you have been. Our sons are constantly bombarded with evils of this world. Satan does not take a holiday. We have been poisoned by degrees, and our sons have been poisoned even more than we have. Satan has chosen to bombard our kids on every front, be it the filth on television, the subtle suggestions found in the media, or the constant exposure to what society esteems as "socially acceptable." The degradation of our society is real, and our kids will be casualties if we do not take the appropriate steps to fortify them.

TAKE COURAGE! God wants you to be successful! The first commandment God gave to Adam and Eve was to multiply and replenish the Earth. Since he commanded it, he is bound to help you rear your children, if you will only try. Fathers, you can connect with your children, they deserve your time and attention. You offer something special, something only a man can provide to his children. I hope and pray this book can help you in your quest to develop the father-son relationship you and your son deserve! May God Bless you in your efforts!

My hope is that if your Father is not or was not that great that you can find something within these pages that you can use. If you had a great father, I hope these pages can help magnify the Father you will become. Your kids need you! I hope this book can help you in your efforts to be a Super Dad - welcome to my world, welcome to ManCamp!

✓ XY Chromosome Combinations Only
See my other books, GirlsCamp - Raising Girls into Women, and FamilyCamp – The Eternal Family for more ideas on other camp adventures).

✓ Be Responsible.

✓ No Electronic Devices and Dad needs to Turn-off the Smart Phone!

✓ Have Fun, ManCamp is Awesome!

Packing List

Do not over-pack! Every little gadget will get in the way! Deviation from this list will only add stress to your ManCamp experience. Be a minimalist, except for clothes and food!

Gear List

- Holy Scriptures
- Journal & Pencil
- Ensign / Friend Magazine
- Sleeping bags (-20 degree is best)
- Tent (3 season is good)
- Axe
- Knife (Bear Grylls Survival Knife is best)
- Matches (waterproof are nice, but optional)
- Paracord / Rope (440 or 550)
- Clothing weather appropriate; (10-20 degrees colder at night while camping)
- Swimming Suits
- Towels
- Sandals
- Work Gloves
- Cooking Pot & Spoon
- Plates, spoons, knives
- Hat
- Durable hiking/walking shoes (steel toe for dad is recommended)
- Warm coats
- Bug Spray
- Sunscreen
- Flashlights
- Toilet Paper
- Cooler
- Backpack
- First Aid Kit
- Cash
- Toiletries (Toothbrushes, Soap, etc.)
- Camera
- Items required for your sons challenge
- Optional: Tarp, Hatchet, BB Gun, Cards, Games, Sling Shot, Metal Cooking Sticks

Food List (Better to over-pack than under-pack)

- o 5-10 Gallons of Water
- o Water bottles or canteens (a flat of recyclable bottles is great)
- o Beans, Salsa & Taco Chips
- o Cereal and Milk (Rice milk (x2) that does not require refrigeration until opened is very handy)
- o Mini carrots and a cucumber
- o Bread, Peanut Butter, Honey (make several sandwiches at home)
- o Granola bars (a few boxes)
- o Smores (Marshmallows, Chocolate Bars, and Graham Crackers)
- o Hot Dogs (frozen) & Buns (Tip: If you pack what I prescribed above, you will not need to buy ice to keep anything cool. Freeze the hotdogs and they should be thaw when it is time to eat them. I advise putting them in an extra Ziploc bag to keep them from leaking.)
- o Cobs of Corn
- o Ziploc sandwich bags

Weeks/Months Before:
o   Read the book "Hatchet," by Gary Paulsen, at night with your son
o   Watch the movie "A Cry in the Wild," rated [PG] released in 1990.
o   Other great novels can be found in the "High Sierra Adventure Series" with titles, "The Legend of the Great Grizzly," "Cougar Chase," "Setting the Trap," and "Mountaintop Rescue."

10 Days Before:
o   Read and Review ManCamp (this book) and be prepared for your son's challenge/reward.
o   Vehicle Check (tires –tread & pressure, oil, coolant etc.)
o   Layout your camping gear, and visit the store to purchase what you are missing
o   Do your laundry
o   Get cash from your bank as most campsites are pay via drop box envelope, and don't make change (20-$1, 5-$5, 5-$10, 5-$20).
o   Select your camp location. Print a map to the camping location. Some parks allow you to book a site in advance, some do not, and the weekends are always the busiest. I recommend a Tuesday through Thursday camp if at all possible, not near a long weekend.
  • http://www.recreation.gov/
  • Ask a worker at the local camping supplies store
  • Ask other locals where they like to camp
  • Assemble a time capsule

Optional (Geocaching Adventure)
✓   Download the geocaching app from Groundspeak Inc. ($10 last time I checked) onto your smartphone if you have one, or get a cheap GPS device. (Global Positioning Device)
✓   Register at www.geocaching.com, please say that raisingboysintomen referred you, and locate a few spots that you can attempt to find while on your camp. There are hundreds, and your son will feel like it is buried treasure. If you don't locate any near your camp location, you can locate one or two near the road on your way to your ManCamp location. There are a few rules of geocaching, so please visit geocaching.com to learn more, prior to doing any treasure hunting.
✓   If you are a beginner, find a geocache near your home prior to attempting this at camp. I advise doing this alone, prior to taking your son, to ensure the cache is intact. You want his first geocache experience to be a positive one.
✓   Find a few geocaches near the location you will be camping. You can plan your hike to one of them on day 2 or 3 if you like.

The Day Before:
✓   Prepare your daypack (See Day 2 of Itinerary)
✓   Pack your Clothing & Load Gear into your vehicle
✓   Gas your vehicle on your way home from work
✓   Grocery Store – Buy your food and put it in a cooler
✓   Make a bunch of peanut butter and honey sandwiches (Ziploc bags).
✓   GET A GOOD NIGHTS SLEEP, you're going to need it.

Day 1

7:00	a.m.	Arise, morning prayers
8:00	a.m.	Final Preparations • Final Gear Check • Money Check • Kiss Momma good-bye • Family Scripture and Prayer (prayer for safety) said by Momma
9:00	a.m.	Depart for your campsite (Tip: Plan to arrive around noon or 1:00 pm. This is when most people are leaving a site from the night before, and it will usually result in you getting the pick of all the available spots)
9:15	a.m.	Use this time on the road to talk to your son, praise him, and tell him how excited you that you are on ManCamp together. Take the time to stop and get a chocolate bar at a gas station. Point out any wild life that you see on the drive, and ask him to keep his eye's peeled for wildlife, especially cougars, wolves, and bears. Let him tell you about school, or play, or whatever is going on in his life. Ask him questions about things he is interested in and let him do a lot of the talking. Take this opportunity to praise him. Ex. You- "Thanks for coming to ManCamp with me; it is awesome to have you come!" Him- "Yah." You- "I am really excited to see what kind of camp spot we are going to get, and if there are bears where we are headed. Him- "Yah." You- "Keep your eyes peeled for wildlife, especially wolves, cougars and bears on the way there ok, if you see some let me know right away ok?" Him- "Ok." You- "So how is 3rd grade going?" Him- "Good" You- "What are your favorite subjects?" Him- "Gym, Science, Art." You "Cool, I used to like Gym a lot too. What do you usually do at recess?" Him- "Kickball" You- "That sounds fun, what positions do you like to play?" Him- "I am the pitcher some of the time, outfield some of the time, and 2nd base some of the time." You- "Which one is your favorite?" Him- "I like to be the pitcher?" You- "Have you ever caught the ball in the air to get someone out? I used to love to do that." Him- "Yeah, last time I caught it and I got their best guy out. It was awesome…" Keep letting him tell you about his life. He will open up to you if you let him. There is no greater way to build the relationship than that. You have already made some major deposits to your relationship bank account on the way to ManCamp!
1:00	p.m.	Arrive at your camping location • Pick your spot (shade and sunlight are factors to consider, as well as proximity to facilities - water, outhouses etc. There is no one perfect camp spot; you have to figure out what works for you.)
1:15	p.m.	Lunch • Drink (Tip: Remember to drink a lot of water! Nature should call every few hours at a minimum while you are camping. Failure to drink will result in you wasting time, and being grouchy, because you are not thinking clearly and your brain is dehydrated, so

		drink, drink, drink every 20 minutes)
		▪ Unload Gear (Tip: There are less bugs in the heat of the day, so get all your work done early)
		▪ Set up Tent
		▪ Roll out Sleeping Bags
		▪ Pay your Campsite Fees (usually $10-$30 per night)
		▪ Set-up water station with soap bar
3:00	p.m.	Review your son's challenges, and assign him jobs to help him fulfill the requirements.
3:15	p.m.	Gather a lot of wood for a fire, work with your son! (While you are at it, find a great cooker stick / fire bug stick for you and your boy)
5:00	p.m.	Help your son build the fire (this is probably in his challenge)
6:00	p.m.	Supper (Hot Dogs or Tupperware containers you packed)
7:00	p.m.	Pile the wood necessary to make the morning fire.
7:45	p.m.	Smores (Roasted marshmallow & chocolate slice pressed between 2 graham wafers)
8:15	p.m.	Spiritual Lesson from Dad and his testimony. As the spirit directs, you might invite your son to share his feelings and testimony (See the Spiritual Lessons at the back)
8:30	p.m.	Plan tomorrow's adventure, and challenges to be completed (hiking, swimming in a stream, geocaching. You should store all food safely in a vehicle or hung in a tree. Also, place your 5 gallon container of water on the ground, as it will chill it overnight, also a great trick for small milk containers if wildlife is scarce)
8:45	p.m.	Bathroom visit, Bed time
9:00	p.m.	Prayers and conversation while in sleeping bags. (This is another opportunity to chat and wrestle, don't let it pass you by. Ask a lot of questions and let your son talk. Flashlight tag is a great game too)

Day 2

6:00	a.m.	Arise, morning prayers
6:15	a.m.	Light morning fire (Tip: If you take a piece of wood approx. the size of your forearm and shove it as deep into the ground, leaving about 5" exposed, where your fire was the night before and leave it alone for about 15 minutes, you will not even need to relight the fire, it will self-ignite.)
6:30	a.m.	Cereal Breakfast
6:45	a.m.	Morning scripture, offer a small lesson (3-5 minutes max, see ManCamp scriptures)
7:00	a.m.	Review Challenges with your son, and Plan (Plan what you would like to do for your hike adventure. You perhaps planned to find a geocache, a spring, a stream, a mountain, no matter your adventure, watch the weather and plan accordingly. If it looks like rain, you may want to plan a smaller adventure, or return to civilization and attend a visitor's tour of the park. Plan to have a positive experience, improvise your plan if necessary).
9:00	a.m.	Gather wood for evening fire.
10:00	a.m.	Morning Snack and Drink
10:15	a.m.	Pack your daypack for your hike. The contents will differ based on the activity you have chosen, but I recommend: ▪ ManCamp Book, Spiritual Lesson items (if needed) ▪ Sling Shot ▪ Swimming Suit, Sandals, Towel ▪ 3-4 Water Bottles ▪ Pre-made sandwiches ▪ Small first aid kit ▪ Knife ▪ 25' Paracord ▪ Sunscreen, Bug Spray
10:30	a.m.	Put out morning fire and begin hike
12:15	p.m.	Lunch

12:45	p.m.	Exploration of the Area (Your spot might be a small stream, a mountain top, a fresh water spring, or a nature spot.)
1:15	p.m.	Spiritual Lesson from Dad (See Spiritual Lessons Section of this book)
1:30	p.m.	Fun at the location (You might want to swim in the stream, climb in the area, or perhaps you planned a geocache search for this time, you might also help your son pass off a challenge at this time, or you could just relax in the shade, no matter what, be sure to have some fun with your son. I always have a slingshot shooting competition during this time)
2:45	p.m.	Begin Hike Back to your camping location.
4:15	p.m.	Arrive back at your base camp
4:30	p.m.	Gather wood for next morning's fire (By now you are probably feeling pretty exhausted, hang in there, you will retire early again tonight).
5:00	p.m.	BB Gun / Sling-shot shoot-off. (Your son will not want to stop when it is time to prepare supper, so this is a good opportunity to let him do it by himself, if you deem him ready, and has learned all the proper safety measures. You are also showing him that you trust him).
5:30	p.m.	Suppertime (ManSupper – Beans, Salsa, Taco Chips, Let your son light the fire if at all possible, it may also fill one of his challenge requirements)
6:30	p.m.	Plan the activities you would like to do for the next day.
7:00	p.m.	Smores (Roasted marshmallow & chocolate slice pressed between 2 graham wafers)
7:15	p.m.	Spiritual Lesson from Dad and his testimony. As the spirit directs, you might invite your son to share his feelings and testimony (See the Spiritual Lessons at the back).
8:30	p.m.	Bathroom Visit and Bedtime
9:00	p.m.	Prayers and conversation while in sleeping bags. Another opportunity to chat and wrestle, don't let it pass you by. Ask a lot of questions and let your son talk. Flashlight tag is a great game too.

Day 3
(If your camp is more than 3 days, generally repeat Day 2, if not see below)

6:00	a.m.	Arise, morning prayers
6:15	a.m.	Light morning fire
6:30	a.m.	Cereal Breakfast
6:45	a.m.	Morning scripture, offer a small lesson (3-5 minutes max, see ManCamp scriptures)
7:00	a.m.	Review Challenges with your son, if there are any outstanding challenges, plan to finish them this morning. It is also time for your son to complete a journal entry about the ManCamp. Help him with his descriptions; you may need to be his scribe. Spend a solid hour on this. (Journals are available on my website)
7:30	a.m.	Pack-up, air-out, and dry-out tent and sleeping bags, Load into your vehicle. (Tip: Doing this in the cool of the morning is much more pleasant than after 9 a.m. when the heat of the day sets in).
8:00	a.m.	Clean the campsite (garbage pickup)
8:30	a.m.	Challenges or Leisure by the morning fire.
10:15	a.m.	Morning Snack and Drink
11:00	a.m.	Head for home. Plan to find one more geocache on the way home. (On the way home, ask your son a lot of questions, let him talk, you be the listener and inquirer).
12:30	p.m.	Burger Place and a Giant Ice-cream Cone
1:00	p.m.	Head for home
2:00	p.m.	Arrive Home and Unload
2:30	p.m.	Listen to the Stories they tell their Mom
3:30	p.m.	Record the Experience in your Journal
6:00	p.m.	Go develop some photos of the camp! Do this the first night back, otherwise, days turn into months, months into years…and you ManCamp Journal will not have the photos it needs to have! GO DO IT!

Preparation

Prior to embarking or planning your ManCamp, you should prepare yourself with the requisite spiritual knowledge, and requisite survival skills to have a successful experience. The old adage goes, if you fail to plan, you plan to fail.

Challenges

Each year, my boys are given a series of challenges. Each year they get progressively more difficult. Though I do not ever complete a task for my son, I make it as easy for him to complete as possible, thereby ensuring his success. In each section, you will find an age range, and a series of challenges/tasks that may be accomplished. Each challenge also has a reward which is given when the tasks have been accomplished. Modify as you see fit, add to, take from, but develop your own system, one that works for you.

If the weather does not cooperate (ie. It rains for 2 days) you can allow your son to complete all his challenges when you return home. There are a lot of local parks where all these challenges can be completed.

Relationship Bank Account
If the concept of an emotional relationship bank account is foreign to you, you will need to understand the concept to develop your own ManCamp. The concept is quite simple. Essentially, we all use emotional currency with each other, sometimes we make deposits (ManCamp, compliments, hugs etc.), and sometimes we make withdrawals (yelling at your son, a smug look of disapproval, etc.). Much like a conventional bank account, the emotional relationship bank account needs to have a lot more deposits than withdrawals, so as you read this book, keep in mind that it was written to help you make deposits. The key purpose of ManCamp is to make major deposits to your son's relationship bank account.

Rewards

Please note that each year's rewards build on the previous years; they are not repurchased each year. Your son may not be ready for a pocket knife at 6, so perhaps you could move that to 7or 8. Your wife might not like firearms, so perhaps you will have to come up with an incentive that makes sense for your son based on his interests.

Journal

Each year at ManCamp your son should complete a small journal entry. The journal entry ties to age appropriate topics based on age appropriate questions. These fall under three categories which are, Mental, Physical and Spiritual. Leather journals are available on my website, or you can visit your local dollar store for a small journal. I recommend a 5x7 or 6x9 with at least 100 pages. On the first page of your son's new journal, write, ManCamp, Your Son's Name, son of Your Name as shown below in the example:

- MANCAMP -   **AUSTIN GEORGE HAMILTON**   **SON OF**   **DAVID GEORGE HAMILTON**

Setting it up this way makes it feel a little like Moroni, son of Mormon don't you think? On the second thru fifth pages, take a moment to write a thoughtful message to your son (see small sample below). Let him know that you have faith in the Lord, and that if he will put his trust in God, he will find happiness in this life. A small testimony might also be appropriate.

A simple written message and testimony might read as follows:

"You are a fine son. There are few things make a dad prouder than a son like you. I look forward to seeing you grow, and become a man. I hope you chose to live a life faithful to the commandments of God. Your Father in Heaven loves you. I love you. Over the past few years I have watched you grow with all the pride a father can have. I like playing guys and cars with you. You have a really good imagination. You have been given many spiritual gifts and I have already seen you use them. You share your testimony with others whenever you set a good example and choose the right. Your Mommy has also seen what a good boy you are, and we are very happy you are a part of our family. We are very blessed to have you! I can't wait to see you grow in the gospel, and gain a testimony of your own. ManCamp has been a lot of fun, but I hope we can be close forever, even when you are a teenager. I can't wait to see you develop your talents and become a man.

As your Father, there are a few things that I want you to know, that I know. I know that there is a loving Father in Heaven, and that He created a plan for you to return to live with him. He sent his son Jesus Christ to atone for the sins of all mankind, this includes you and I. The Holy Ghost can be your constant companion if you will live worthily. I have read the scriptures and attest that they contain the truth and the fullness of the gospel of Jesus Christ. You will be happy if you abide their teaching and the teachings of the spirit. The fullness of the gospel has been restored, as well as the power of God which you will one day hold called the Holy Priesthood. You have been the source of great happiness for me, and I pray you will one day be able to have a family sealed to you, as I have been sealed to your mother and you. Choose wisely the young lady you marry, and take her to the temple. Treat her like your princess always! As you serve others you will find great happiness in this life. Take the life and teachings of the Savior Jesus Christ as your guide and example. Heed the promptings of the Spirit, and consecrate your every effort to his Kingdom. There is a prophet on the Earth today, listen to his council, as they are from God. You are a son of God. I hope you chose to live a life faithful to the commandments of God, all your life, but if you should stray, remember that the Lord Jesus Christ has provided the way for you to repent, and be white as snow again. Your Father in Heaven loves you, your mother loves you, and I love you.

Your best pal, Dad."

Scribe

Until he is probably 9-10ish, you will probably have to record his ideas for him. You will find details of each journal entry later in this book on the summary pages for each age. Be vigilant in keeping this record, as he will have it forever. It can be done at home when your son is younger, you may even use a voice recorder to get his exact words, but be sure to write them in his book, as this will be a book he will treasure forever! Leave a page at the end of each year to paste in a photograph! Remember to take pictures!

Spiritual Lessons – BEAR YOUR TESTIMONY!
Alma 30:44

"... all things denote there is a God; yea, even the earth, and all things that are upon the face of it, yea, and its motion, yea, and also all the planets which move in their regular form do witness that there is a Supreme Creator."

While you are out enjoying nature, be sure to stop and take a deep breath once in a while, and admire the beauty of God's creations. ManCamp is the perfect opportunity to tell your sons about what is most

15

important in life. Your beliefs may differ from mine, but lessons of character and integrity are of paramount importance.

Some of these lessons may not be suitable for your son, some may not be, "your style," but I hope and pray you can take something from the lessons below. Please tailor them to your needs, and revise them as you see fit, but please take the opportunity to talk to your son!

Ensign, November 1985
(Worthy Fathers, Worthy Sons)
"In the Book of Mormon, faithful fathers constantly bore their testimonies to their sons. "Remember that these sayings are true, and also that these records are true," King Benjamin testified to his sons. (Mosiah 1:6.) Alma bore witness to his son Helaman saying, "I do know; and the knowledge which I have is of God." (Alma 36:26.) ...the Book of Mormon, which is the most correct book on earth, demonstrates that the major responsibility for teaching our sons the great plan of the Eternal Father—the Fall, rebirth, Atonement, Resurrection, Judgment, eternal life—rests with fathers. It should be done individually as well as in the family. It should be preached and discussed so our children will know the commandments. It should be done from their youth up—and often." – President Ezra Taft Benson

PREPARATION:

- ✓ Pray, Fast (the Sunday before ManCamp), and Study your Scriptures. Ask the Lord to bless you as you seek to connect your son to his gospel.
- ✓ See Spiritual Lessons – A Mountain Stream, The Mountain, and A Campfire.
- ✓ Check the website www.raisingboysintomen.com to see if there are any videos you may need to watch to prepare.
- ✓ Invite mommy to say a prayer right before you leave for ManCamp, asking Heavenly Father to keep her boys in safety.

CHALLENGE:

- ✓ Gather sticks for the fire.
- ✓ Invite him to say his prayers every morning and night. Help him learn what to say.

REWARD:

- ✓ Firebug stick
- ✓ (Keep a sharp eye on your son! Caution: Please monitor your boys! They can land face first in the flames, they can start a forest fire, and they can poke out an eye, just to list a few of the potential hazards!)
- ✓ Survival Bracelet with a shackle that has a whistle. (Instructions on how to make one are at the end of this chapter, or they can be purchased on my website)
- ✓ A small dollar store flashlight with carabineer to clip onto his pants.

JOURNAL ENTRY: (you will need to scribe for him in his journal)

- ✓ Mental – Have you been working on your ABC's, and your Counting?
- ✓ Physical – Do you like to run and play until you get tired?
- ✓ Spiritual – What is Jesus like?
- ✓ Fun - My favorite thing that happened at ManCamp was…
- ✓ Photo Page

NOTES:

Gather Sticks

Show your little boy what types of sticks you are wanting in a pile, and show him where to form the pile, this will set him up for success. As your boy gather the sticks, congratulate him on the good job he is doing, and act impressed. Periodically go to the pile he has made and pull a few sticks and tell him how well you think -- that stick, or this stick will burn.

"Good job Buddy! You are working really hard!"
"Wow, you are a really good worker man."
"Nice job, that pile of sticks is great, you pick good ones."
"Wow that stick will burn really well, good eye, pal!"

Even a small job like this can build your sons confidence, and will make him feel like a part of a bigger project. At the conclusion, congratulate him on the great pile, and what a good job he has done. Immediately go and find a good fire-poking stick, and set it by the fire pit, and tell them that it is for him to use later. Next get a survival bracelet with your family colors, and put it on him. Show him how his bracelet matches yours, and his older brother(s), if he has any, and tell him it is a survival bracelet, and show him how the whistle works.

Relationship Bank Account

You taught him a great lesson in fire building, and it only took 5 minutes. He will be convinced that ManCamp is awesome by now, and you will have him looking forward to every year thereafter! Boys naturally want to do things that "big-guys" do, so why not let him benefit and grow by letting him participate. Remember, the camp isn't about—getting stuff done, it is about your son's growth, and you facilitating that growth. Think back on someone that built you up; did they entrust you with some sort of responsibility, and then congratulated you for a job well-done, perhaps a coach, a boss, your dad, or your uncle? Congratulations! You have just made a major deposit to your relationship bank account! Your son will already be excited for the fire, but you just deposited about $500 emotional bucks. When he goes home, he will tell his mom about the sticks he gathered, and will be the new family resident authority on the best small sticks that burn.

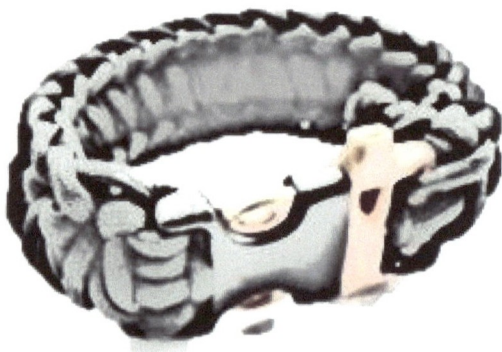

Survival Bracelet Instructions (can be purchased on my website)

Step 1 – Get some paracord, a lighter, and a knife.

Step 2 – Cut a length suitable to your wrist size, and tie a knot on the end, picking your new family colors may be the hardest part.

Step 3 – Cut another length about 5' or so, better more than less, so you don't run out.

Step 4 – If you are going to get fancy, get two pieces of 2.5' in length, cut and melt them together.

Step 5 – Here is the basic cobra stitch…do not get frustrated! This takes a while to master. I use a karabiner to hold the top loop to a bar or handle to a cabinet drawer to hold it in place.

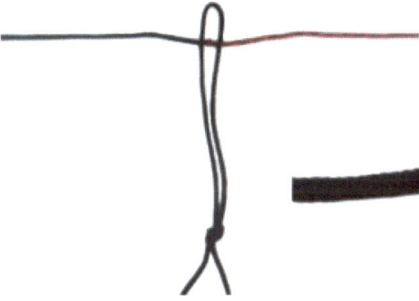

Spiritual Lesson
A Mountain Stream

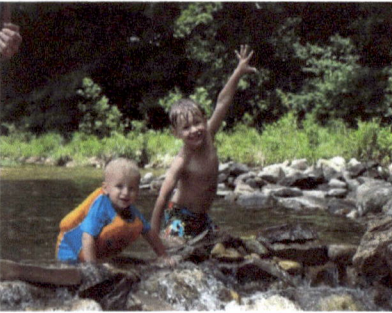

On the second day of ManCamp, I plan a hike (according to the ages of my boys, and what is comfortable and reasonable) and find a good place to jump into a mountain stream. I bring a pack with lunch, sunscreen, water bottles, slingshots, pocket knives, etc. We spend the better part of the day (3-4 hours from 11-3 pm) in the shade, in the stream, in the grass, and in the woods. As the day draws on, it is all about discovering where minnows hide, where squirrels live, where the best log to sit can be found. It is all about discovery.

I visit the stream and gather about 2 dozen smooth stones, an about two dozen rough stones. I find a nice place beside the stream and have my sons gather around.

I begin with a few congratulations to each of the boys for braving the cold stream, for their climbing abilities, for their hawk-eye in seeing nature, etc. I like to find a few things to praise each boy about. Then I start a short lesson about nature. My lesson goes something like this, "Boys, a stream is like the power of God. It runs without stopping and has an effect on all the stones. Each of the riverbed rocks are like us." Then I pull out the stones that I gathered previously. "See this rock, it is really smooth. It probably took the stream a thousand years to smooth the rough edges off of this stone, and now look how smooth it is. Just like the stream smooth's stones, living God's commandments can smooth us to a fine smooth polish. Now look at this stone (rough stone). See how it has some rough edges. Sin, bad habits, unkindness, they can be the rough edges some people have. Just like this rock, it has rough edges, do you think that the stream can smooth the rough edges?" My son's respond affirmatively. "With the help of Jesus Christ, we can repent of our wrongs, and God can polish us smooth. That is how God can refine us too. If we give our Father in Heaven time to refine us, we too can be smooth stones. What types of things do you think this stone needs help with?" Then I hand the boys a stone. My eldest son says something like, "being dishonest can be made to honest." I say "that is right," then I say "toss it into the stream, and let the rough dishonest stone become a smooth honest stone with God's help." Then my middle son, responds something like, "avoiding pictures of naked people so we can be pure." I respond, "Good, toss it into the stream." My youngest son says, "Choose to obey mom right away so she doesn't get upset." I say, "Yes, Heavenly Father can help us be

20

obedient to our mother, toss in your stone." The rocks start flying by this point into the stream with comments like, "stop saying bad words," and "be kind to the next door neighbor." After the stones are thrown in the stream, I get their attention back, and offer these words. "Boys, I know that your Heavenly Father wants you to be as smooth stones, that your sins can be smoothed over with God's help, just like the stream can smooth a stone, so too can Heavenly Father smooth you, as you use the Atonement of his son Jesus Christ, in the name of Jesus Christ, Amen.

Isaiah 1: 18-20
18 Come now, and let us reason together, saith the Lord: though your sins be as scarlet, they shall be as white as snow; though they be red like crimson, they shall be as wool.
19 If ye be willing and obedient, ye shall eat the good of the land:
20 But if ye refuse and rebel, ye shall be devoured with the sword: for the mouth of the Lord hath spoken it.

A Campfire
While we sit around the campfire, I remind my boys that a fire is like a testimony of truth in the Savior Jesus Christ and God the Father. If we light a small fire, and leave it alone, it will burn out and die. If we let wind get to it, and if we allow rain to fall upon it, it can extinguish our testimony. We need to protect our testimony. We can help our testimony, like a fire, by putting on more wood on the small flame. As we keep the commandments of God, as we honor our parents, as we read our scriptures, as we pray to him often, we can put sticks on the fire, and make our blaze strong. Should we put too much wood on at once? No, that is why God has told us that a man should not run faster than he has strength. We need to carefully add wood until the flame is able to consume it, and the more we do that, the brighter the light, and stronger the flame. The more we share God's truth with others the brighter our flame. Once our flame is large, should we leave it unattended? No! We need to continually help our testimony grow by doing what is right, and by living the commandments of God, by choosing the right, and by living up to our potential.

A Seed
As we are walking I show them a small seed at the base of a large tree. I ask them if they think the seed is very valuable. Ask them why they feel the way they do. Some boys will see it as valuable, some will not, it really does not matter what they respond, both answers will allow you to lead to the appropriate teaching. I then ask them to look up to the tall trees surrounding us. This seed is like us, we are small right now, but with God's blessing upon us, we can grow to magnificent trees. We can become spiritual giants. Some trees grow small, some grow medium, some grow large, and it is up to us what type of tree we want to be. We can grow crooked, we can grow sideways, but we will grow. It is up to us to choose to grow straight, and by keeping the commandments, we are able to grow as Heavenly Father wants us

21

to grow. He can help us reach heights we never thought possible. Then I ask them, if this tree was out in a field somewhere, would wind have more effect on it? Notice how closely the trees grow, and when the wind comes, they do not have to only rely on themselves, because if they have grown as they should have grown, their roots will be so intertwined with the rest of the trees around, that they will be able to hold them, and be held by them. In fact, the entire forest works together. The roots of all the trees can represent parents, friends, siblings, ecclesiastical leaders, family, and so forth. You see, God never leaves us to do this life all alone; He has prepared people around us to help us. If you are a large tree, your roots have the ability to reach out to a tiny tree off by itself, and to hold on to it, and to help it to grow, and to support it when the winds of life come upon it. Just like trees, we can reach out to others and offer caring support. The bigger we grow, the more good we can do, so it is important to live up to your potential, and to help others.

The Mountain

It is important to be like a mountain. Rains come, winds blow, and lightning strikes, but the mountain does not fear the elements. As children of God, we are the greatest of all his creations. In life, there will be storms, maybe we lose a job, maybe we lose a parent, maybe we lose our business, maybe we lose our way. Maybe we sin, and a small chip of the mountain rolls off the top. Is the mountain worth less because of a small stone? We are like the mountain, no matter what we do in this life, we are children of God. It is He that oversees all. It is He that created us. If we sin, we lose a small chip off the top, but we are still children of God. Our value in His sight will never change. When life's winds blow upon us, when sin enters our life, when we lose sight of the mountain because we are too busy watching for falling rocks, we have lost the view Heavenly Father has of us. Through his Son's grace, we may be restored. Through his Son's grace, we may be made whole. Life's troubles are a passing moment. But just as a storm passes through the mountains, so too, life's troubles pass, and there is a bright day beyond the storm clouds. Take courage, God created you, and will help you every step of the way. You are the mountain; do not fear a storm cloud! You are a son of God; do not let life's set-backs tear you down. Be solid, take courage, you are sons of the Almighty God.

Proverbs 22:6
Train up a child in the way he should go: and when he is old, he will not depart from it.

PREPARATION:

- ✓ Pray, Fast (the Sunday before ManCamp), and Study your Scriptures. Ask the Lord to bless you as you seek to connect your son to his gospel.
- ✓ Research the story about the boys who, under the direction of the Prophet Joseph Smith while residing in Nauvoo, were tasked with "whistling and whittling." Ask your little boy which stick they would pick to whittle if they were assigned by the prophet to keep an eye on a rough character.
- ✓ Prior to the camp, tell your son how excited you are that he will be earning his pocket knife this year. Remind him that he will be able to use his new knife while at camp while he is on your knee, and that for the 1st year it will be in mom's jewelry box for safe keeping but that he can look at it whenever he wants.
- ✓ Check the website www.raisingboysintomen.com to see if there are any videos you may need to watch to prepare.
- ✓ Invite mommy to say a prayer right before you leave for ManCamp, asking Heavenly Father to keep her boys in safety.

CHALLENGE:

- ✓ Set a rabbit trap
- ✓ Gather sticks & Light the first fire of camp
- ✓ Invite him to be baptized when he turns 8
- ✓ Learn to estimate the remaining daylight time in the day

REWARD:

- ✓ A folding pocket knife

JOURNAL:

- ✓ Mental – Why should you do your best in all subjects at school, not only the ones you enjoy?
- ✓ Physical – Why is it important to eat lots of fruits and vegetables?
- ✓ Spiritual – How can saying frequent prayers, including morning and evening prayers, help you grow closer to your Heavenly Father?
- ✓ Fun - My favorite thing that happened at ManCamp was…
- ✓ Photo Page

NOTES:

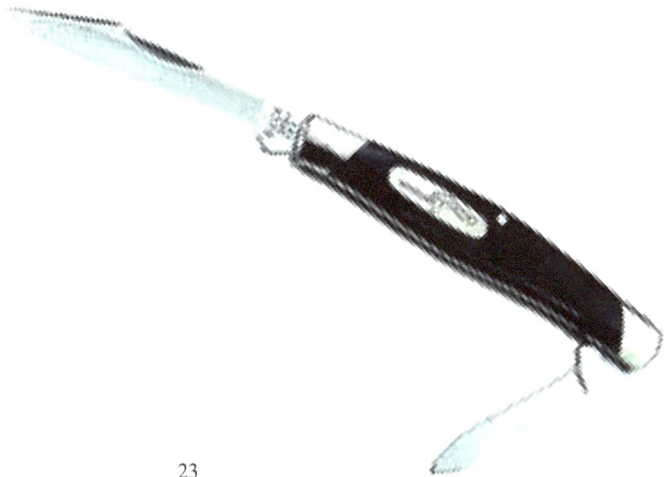

Rabbit and Squirrel Traps

(Please watch the video on my website prior to attempting this. Go to www.raisingboysintomen.com)
It is important that you have the trap mastered before you have your son attempt to set it. Please realize, the trap is "spring loaded," so you should take precaution not to get flicked in the eye by a small yearling tree. It is a very basic trap. You can purchase it on my website with instructions, or you can engineer one of your own.

The Noose and Peg Trap

As your boy sets his trap, and you allow him to test it, he will light up with glee! Having the trap set will be half the fun of this ManCamp. Please remind your son that rabbits are smart, and that the trap might be set

Post stuck FIRMLY into the ground.

for months before a rabbit is caught. In reality, the trap is very basic, and you would need to set a few dozen traps, in a highly populated rabbit area to catch one. Your son does not need to know that, but you should emphasize how proud you are, of your son in setting the trap. The entire time you are at ManCamp, you will be quite entertained seeing your son checking the trap every few minutes. If you catch and injure an animal, you should plan on killing it and eating it, but the likelihood of your son's first trap actually capturing something is very unlikely. Below are drawings of rabbit tracks and rabbit droppings, in case you don't know how they appear.

Step 1	Gather the materials you will need: 2 sticks (approx. 8'' in length and 2'' in diameter) 8 feet of rope A hammer
Step 2	Notch the sticks (about 1" from the end of each stick carve a small angle inward in the shape of the number 7. Each stick should have a number 7 carved into it, and they should be fitted together so they clasp together as shown in image above)
Step 3	Carve a ¼" groove all the way around one of the sticks
Step 4	Leave approx. 3' of slack on one end of the rope, then tie the rope tightly into the grove on the top stick.
Step 5	Tie a slip knot on the other end of the rope and make a small 6" diameter noose.
Step 6	Locate a small game trail, look for rabbit poop piles and tall grass, then locate a small yearling tree 5' tall along the trail.
Step 7	Tie the loose end to the top of the yearling and intertwine it with a solid branch.
Step 8	Bend the yearling toward the trail until the spring is highly tense. Then measure where the notched stick touches the game trail.
Step 9	Hammer the loose stick into the location where the other notched stick touched the game trail.
Step 10	Pull the yearling over and link the 7's notches.
Step 11	Place the noose over the game trail. Use grass, or other small sticks to brace the noose in place.
Step 12	Put logs and debris onto the trail in a V-shape to funnel game toward the trap.

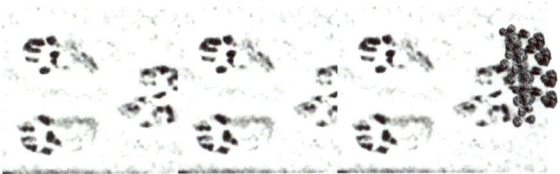

The Figure-4 Trap

The figure-4 trap can be a little trickier than the other trap. Notching the wood and setting up a free falling basket or rock can cause a broken finger very quickly if you are not extremely careful. This trap takes a lot of practice, and I recommend notching your 3 sticks at home before camp if it is your first time. The sticks form a 4, as shown below, and the downward pressure (stored kinetic energy for you science guys) of the falling item holds the trap in place.

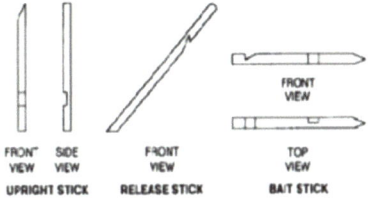

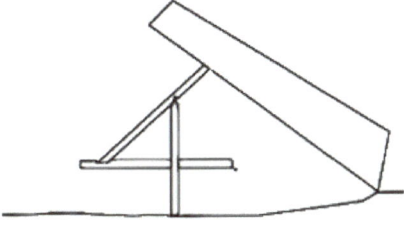

Your son has just had an experience that will build his self-confidence. Another major deposit has been made into the relationship bank account. When he gets home, he will tell his mom about the rabbit trip he set, and the fire he lit. It will be a great opportunity for you to elevate his status and brag about his abilities in front of his mother.

Awarding your son his new Knife

Some people think that 6 years old is too young for a pocket knife, but you will find that your son is able to handle the responsibility, if you let him. Be sure that he is under close personal supervision, and teach him how to whittle wood. Sitting while whittling on dads knee is mandatory! Be sure to tout his awesome success every few minutes for a few hours, and then about once an hour for the remainder of the camp. Every few minutes, I pat my son on the back and tell him how proud I am of him. I then give him another stern warning to be very careful with his new knife.

Lighting the Fire

Having a box of strike anywhere matches is mandatory. Demonstrate how to hold the match carefully to your son. Light 2 or 3 to show him how it is done. Emphasize that it is kind of a hard thing to do, and that he might have some trouble. Reassure him of your confidence in his ability to do it, and that he can try a lot of times if he does not get it the first time. The exhilaration of lighting the fire will be an immediate reward to your son's self-confidence. Entrusting your son to light the first fire has taught him that he can contribute and be trusted to do "big-guy," things. When he reflects one day as a grown man, on the few recollections he has from his childhood, lighting the fire at ManCamp will be deeply etched into his brain, and he will remember that you were by his side. All night you can congratulate him on such a fine fire, and how nice it is to be sitting by such a nice flame. Even though you did 99% of the work for it to be a success, he will only remember that he made the fire happen. It is his fire!

Estimating Daylight

To estimate the remaining daylight minutes at any given time after approximately 2:00 p.m. put your fingers together as shown below. Each adult digit (medium build) represents about 15 minutes. If you have large or small hands, adjust accordingly. The hand of a 6 year-old with the thumb is usually about an hour. Do not look at the sun, but place your hand in the air so the forefinger is directly under the base of the sun and count hand over hand to the horizon.

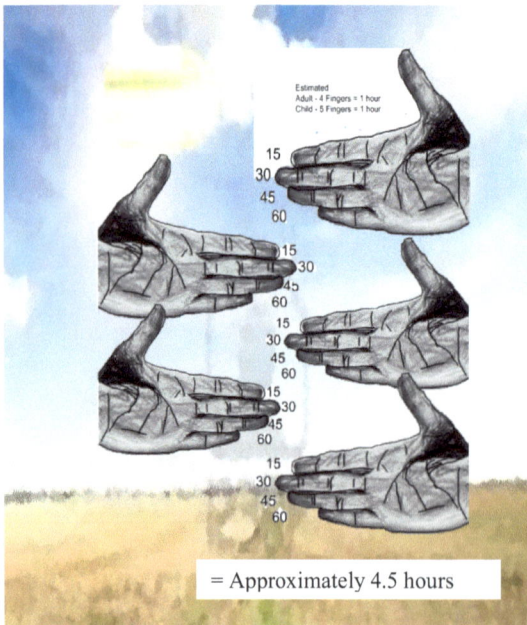

= Approximately 4.5 hours

Spiritual Lessons
Whistling and Whittling Brigade
While sitting by the fire carving for the first time, I like to relay this story. It needs little introduction other

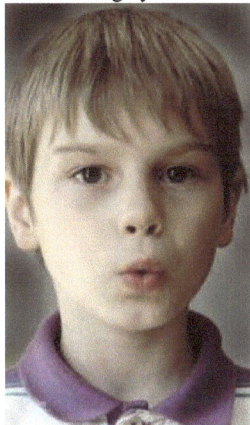

than, " I have a cool story about a bunch of little guys who all had pocket knives who were able to defend and entire city, would you like to hear more? While the Latter-Day Saints were living in Nauvoo, because the town no longer had a charter, it was impossible for the citizens to form a police force. Ruffians began creeping into the town, some with the intention to do families harm. In response to the continual threat of these terrible characters, the Boys of the town formed a brigade. Their mission was to keep an eye on anyone that came to town that was a stranger. They were instructed not to talk to the person at all. All they were supposed to do was follow the person around town and whittle wood while whistling. The bad men wanted to remain unnoticed while they crept about town, but being followed closely by a half dozen boys making a racket while carving wood made it nearly impossible. The last thing a bad guy wants is to be seen by anyone while they commit a crime. The boys made a lasting impact giving the men who kept watch by night a much needed break. Even little guys can make a difference, when there are enough of them."

Joshua 1:9
...Be strong and of a good courage; be not afraid, neither be thou dismayed: for the Lord thy God is with thee whithersoever thou goest.

A Spring of Water

Each year, I take my sons on a short hike to a mountain spring. After a few minutes of exploration, I gather my sons, and stand near the head of the spring. I begin by talking about God's goodness, and how he is like a spring of fresh water. He will quench our thirst when we are in need. God is a fountain of water, that if we drink, we will never thirst again, because what he has to offer will quench our thirst. Just as water quenches the thirst for our body, the teachings of God will quench our spiritual thirst. Just as drinking from this spring will aid your body to subsist for a few more hours, God's grace allows us to subsist from second to second. As we keep God's commandments, and seek to do His will, we will discover his ability to quench our spiritual thirst, and be filled with happiness.

John 14:6
Jesus saith unto him, I am the way, the truth, and the life: no man cometh unto the Father, but by me.

PREPARATION:
- ✓ Pray, Fast (the Sunday before ManCamp), and Study your Scriptures. Ask the Lord to bless you as you seek to connect your son to His gospel.
- ✓ Research the story of David and Goliath as found in the 1st book of Samuel chapter 17. See the spiritual lessons section Standing on the Lord's Side. (You will need a piece of chalk and a slingshot for the lesson.) also see age 6, The Campfire.
- ✓ Check the website www.raisingboysintomen.com to see if there are any videos you may need to watch to prepare.
- ✓ Invite mommy to say a prayer right before you leave for ManCamp, asking Heavenly Father to keep her boys in safety.

CHALLENGE:
- ✓ Build a rabbit trap
- ✓ Build the first fire of camp, and gather sticks
- ✓ Invite him to reaffirm his goal for baptism at 8

REWARD:
- ✓ A sling shot.

JOURNAL:
- ✓ Mental – Why should we study for our classes at school? Should we ever look at another person's answers?
- ✓ Physical – Why is it important to go to bed at a good time? How do we feel when we stay up late, and eat a lot of junk food? Are those the foods Heavenly Father would have us eat?
- ✓ Spiritual – How can reading your scriptures daily help keep you safe from tempting thoughts and actions? What does the spirit feel like?
- ✓ Fun - My favorite thing that happened at ManCamp was…
- ✓ Photo Page

NOTES:

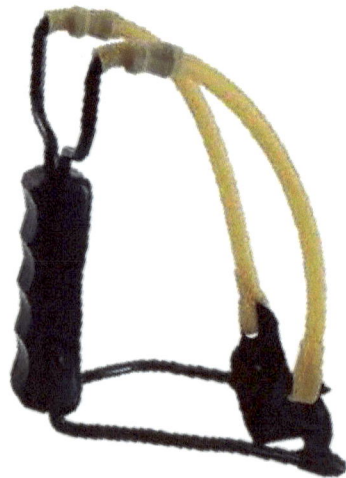

Build a Rabbit Trap

Last year, your son just had to set the trap, this year, he must build it. With the knife he has in his pocket from last year; supervise him in notching the sticks, in grooving one of the sticks, and in tying the knots. Building it can be much more difficult, so encourage, and support, but resist the urge to take over. Remember, it is a time for your son to learn something about himself here, not an opportunity for you to do it for him. You may, however, set him up for a successful experience by prefabricating some of the cuts so he has a pattern. On the sticks that need to be notched, I perform on small cut (see below). It may take him a day or two, and it may take a few attempts, but he will eventually get it. Don't let him give up, encourage him, and show him. Teach him that he can do difficult things, if he will just apply himself and keep with it. He will likely get very frustrated, keep a cool head, and stay positive, and support him. The deeper lesson is at stake. If he feels defeated, move to the next step of, building the fire, and let him have some success there. It will encourage him to complete the trap later. Tell him that it is very difficult to light a good fire, and to get it to burn well, that way, when he accomplishes it, you can brag him up a little, and he will have his complete confidence restored.

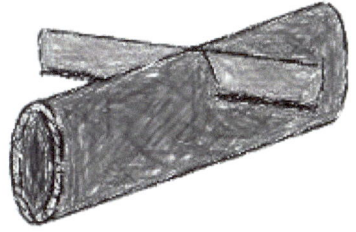

Build a Fire

There are various styles of small starter fires. A couple of the more common are the teepee and the log cabin method. Pictured below are a teepee, and a combination (teepee inside a log cabin). Gather the sticks together, and let him build his fire in the pit. Work beside him, and build your own teepee, or log house. Tell your son that they sometimes fall down, and that it can be tough to get it right. Perhaps even let yours fall before his, and laugh at yourself. Then there will be less pressure on him, seeing that you failed before him. Also, you have taught him the proper way to respond to adversity, not just in building a fire, but in life. Words of affirmation are key at this stage, and consistently tell him what a good job he is doing, and pat him on the back several times.

This year he will learn a lot about himself, and if you have done it correctly, he will have a positive experience, overall, in-spite of some tears. When he gets home, be sure to brag him up to his mom, and let her know that he is a master of fires. This year, he can be trusted to keep that pocket knife in a special place in his room if he prefers, or it can stay in safe keeping in mom's jewelry box. Your son will never forget this year because of the deep emotions he felt, but you have taught him to conquer those feeling, and that if he works hard, he can accomplish anything!

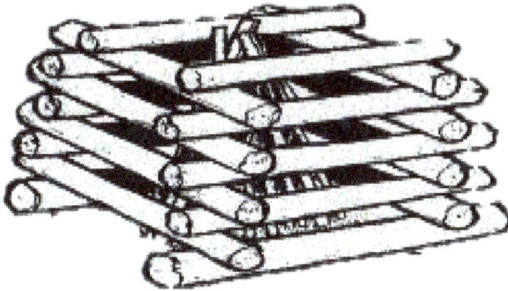

Standing with the Lord (1 Samuel 17)

You will need a piece of chalk, a slingshot, a tape measure, and some round stones. As you are hiking or while you are at a leisure location surrounded by trees start by issuing a challenge. The first one to hit that tree with a throwing stone gets to have the first smore made at camp tonight. As you have fun trying to hit the tree by throwing rocks, it is nice if your son wins, but if he does, make sure it is not obvious that you lost on purpose. When the first challenge is done, tell him it is time to raise the stakes. Get the slingshot from your backpack and take turns trying to hit another tree. After a couple of challenges, take some chalk and go to wide tree in the distance with your son. Use the tape measure to measure 10 feet tall and draw a circle the size of a large watermelon on the trunk of the tree, and put a large capital G above it. Draw crazy eyes, a nose, and a mouth on the trunk. Return to your shooting spot and take turns shooting at the circle on the tree and tell him, "I know a really cool story, but you probably already know it, it is an amazing story. Even if you have heard it, please let me tell you anyway, it might not be exactly the same as you have heard before. You see that circle over there? There was once a boy that shot a sling shot, and in one try could hit that right between the eyes. He was a little older that you are now, but not much. He was only 14 years old, and he was a boy who tended sheep for his family. One day, a wicked army invaded the land to the North and all the grown men were enlisted into military service. Because he was only 14, his dad didn't let him go to defend the country; instead he was put in charge of the whole family herd of sheep. The family lived in a dangerous land, and there were bears everywhere, and there were lions everywhere. While tending the flock, the boy had to camp out by himself in the dark. He had to keep watch day and night. The job of a shepherd is to keep watch all the time. One day, while watching his flock of sheep he saw a lion sneaking up on a little lamb. The boy yelled and shouted and threw sticks but the lion didn't run away, it just stared at the boy and approached the lamb even quicker. They boy cut off the lion as it was feet from the lamb and tackled it. The lion and the boy wrestled, and boy was really scratched up, but in the end, the boy got a hold of the lion's throat and choked it to death with his bare hands. He was a hero, and the flock was saved. Barely recovered the boy practiced throwing his knife, and using it as a weapon, when off in the distance, a giant bear began charging the sheep. The boy ran as fast as he could to save the flock, and was able to cut the bear off before it made it to the lambs. The bear rose onto its two hind legs and growled fiercely. The boy saw his opportunity, and as the bear was returning its balance to all 4's, the boy charged the bear, and rammed the knife deep inside the bear's chest. The knife went in so clean, and so quickly, the bear died instantly. It landed on the boy's leg, and the boy was badly injured, but the bear didn't have sheep for lunch that day. A few days later, the boy's father loaded a small donkey with grain and blankets and told the boy to take it to his older brothers near the front lines of the war. His brothers were mighty men of battle. The boy arrived at the front lines only to see no fighting at all. The war had come to a complete stop. The boy quickly located his older brothers and delivered the supplies as his father had instructed him to do. While unloading the grain, he heard a thunderous shout from the enemy. The boy didn't remember exactly what the man said, but it was something like, 'you men are cowards, come and fight me. I will fight your best soldier. Your God does not exist, a curse upon you and a curse upon your God.' The boy had been taught at a young age to always stand up for God, and wondered how his brothers would let the man say such horrible things. The boy told his brothers he would not listen to such terrible talk another minute. The boy began walking to the front lines

30

only to be stopped by his brothers. The brothers told him the man was a giant, and that no one man could stand up to him. The boy looked his brothers in the eye and told them, as the Lord lives, and as I live, that man will die today. The boy went to a nearby stream and gathered a few rocks. The boy walked quickly out onto the battlefield and directly at the giant. He shouted, 'as the Lord God of Israel lives, the birds will feast upon your flesh this day.' The giant soldier laughed at the boy, because he was so small. The giant charged down the hill at the boy with his spear and a yell that rattled the rocks on the mountain. The boy took a deep breath, put a stone in his sling shot and aimed and fired. The giant was about as far away as that tree and the boy nailed the giant right between the eyes. The giant fell to the Earth. The army of Israel charged the enemy and drove them from the land. That day, the Lord used a small 14 year old boy to do what no man had the courage to do. He used him for his purposes. The Lord will use us if we are willing to let him. We can be like the boy in this story. I think you know this was David and Goliath, but perhaps the story should really be entitled David and the Lord. It really didn't matter that Goliath was 10 feet tall, he could have been an entire army of 20 foot tall men; in the end the Lord side always wins. David showed courage. I have seen you show courage. Maybe you will never have to face a giant, but there are a lot of evils in this world much larger than a giant named goliath. The magazines, the TV, the internet are full of powerful enemies that, like Goliath, seek to destroy you. I want you to know you are a powerful boy. You are like David. You will win as long as you stay on the Lord's side." If during your story he hit the circle congratulate him on his marksmanship. I would make it a point to make sure he hits the circle more times than you. A score of 9-6 or something will be clear enough to let him have the bragging rights back at camp and to his mother later. It will really be rewarding to hear him brag to his mom about how hit Goliath more times than you, and it will be especially great for you to brag about that as well for years to come.

PREPARATION:
- ✓ Pray, Fast (the Sunday before ManCamp), and Study your Scriptures. Ask the Lord to bless you as you seek to connect your son to his gospel.
- ✓ Research and be able to locate the big dipper, little dipper and the North Star. See Spiritual Lesson - Stars.
- ✓ Check the website www.raisingboysintomen.com to see if there are any videos you may need to watch to prepare.
- ✓ Invite mommy to say a prayer right before you leave for ManCamp, asking Heavenly Father to keep her boys in safety.

CHALLENGE:
- ✓ Cook the supper
- ✓ Build the fire
- ✓ Invite him to set a goal to one day hold the Aaronic priesthood, and to start reading his scriptures daily.
- ✓ Use a compass to tell direction & identify the North Star.

REWARD:
- ✓ A BB gun.

JOURNAL:
- ✓ Mental – How can I grow by reading books that have nothing to do with school, and why is it important to learn things not learned in school?
- ✓ Physical – Why is it important to get plenty of regular exercise?
- ✓ Spiritual – How can obeying the law of the fast strengthen my spirit? Why is it important to have a good balance in life of mental, physical, and spiritual things?
- ✓ Fun - My favorite thing that happened at ManCamp was…
- ✓ Photo Page

NOTES:

Cooking the Supper

Domestic skills are very important. The savage man might think that shooting a deer, cutting off a leg, and eating it raw is ideal, but realistically, we need domestic skills. Not only will your son realize the level of difficulty and effort required to prepare a meal, your son will respect the meal preparer in your family. Preparing a hanging tripod is a difficult task, and will require planning, and supervision. You will need a pot with a lid made of cast iron, a wooden or metal cooking spoon, a chain, and a pair of leather gloves. Even if you do not construct a tripod to hold you supper, you can use the metal grill provided over the fire pit at most campgrounds. My typical ManCamp supper is made by mixing a couple of cans of beans, and a bottle of medium salsa. My boys and I try to eat without silverware, and use a bag of Tostito chips to scoop our Man dinner from our bowls. Let your son check the pot frequently; let him know you do not want to eat burnt supper. Remind him to check the pot about every 2 minutes, and to stir it each time he checks. Let your son serve the supper into each bowl. Eating such a basic meal will also help your son appreciate finer feasts offered at home. As you eat, brag on what a great Man meal it is, and how proud you are of his great accomplishment. Even though it is just beans and salsa, with a few chips, the work it took to make it happen will make the grub taste like manna to your son. My sons even ask for man dinner when my wife has girls' night out, and yes it is yummy, but I find it hilarious that they request "Man dinner" over pizza, it cannot be the taste; it must be the memories.

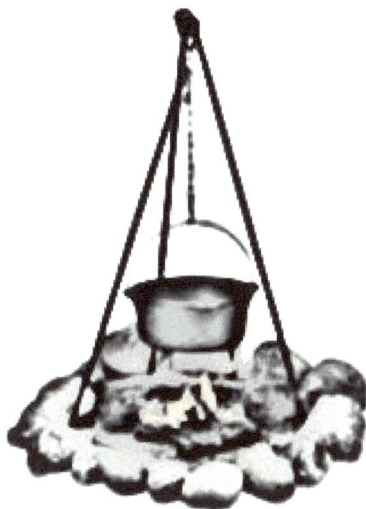

Build the Fire

Your son should be proficient by this point in gathering sticks and building a fire. Turn the responsibility completely over to him at this point. Please ensure he is not wearing a nylon coat or something flammable before you hand him a pack of matches, also be mindful of the surrounding forest, accidents can cost millions. Words of affirmation are key here, let him know how good the sticks he has gathered look, and that you are confident they will burn well. Frequent pats on the back are essential at this point. He might light the fire first match, and it may take the entire box, just be sure to have some extras. If he has tried dozens of times, do not take over. Let him fail a few hundred times if necessary, a box of matches is definitely worth the self-confidence he will have built when the fire is started.

Using a Compass

Using a compass can be really simple. Hold the compass flat on your palm. Align the red arrow and the N. It is pointing North. There are many other ways to tell direction in nature, but here are a few of the easy ones.

- Geese Fly South in the fall and North in the spring.
- Find an old half rotted tree that is still alive. Moss has a tendency to grow on the North side of such bark at a quicker rate than any other direction.
- Depending on the season and your latitude variation may occur, but in general, the sun rises in the East and Sets in the West.
- If it is nighttime, find the little dipper, the North Start is the brightest in the handle.

Generally fly South in Fall and North in Spring.

The North Star

N

Spiritual Lessons
The Stars

By the evening campfire, take a moment to walk into the darkness and view the stars in the heavens. On the right night they will illuminate the view. Lay a blanket on the ground away from the fire, and watch the stars with your son. Here is a sample of some of the things you can say and ask. The Book of Mormon teaches us many things about the heavens. Alma said that all things that are upon the face of the land, the motion of the planet do attest there is a Supreme Creator, and that creator is the Lord Jesus Christ (Alma 30:44). How many stars can you count? It is pretty amazing that God can govern this whole universe at the same time don't you think?

After we die, we will go to the spirit world. We will be there for a little while, until we are resurrected. That means we will receive our bodies back in a perfected form. Much later we will be judged of our works in this life. Jesus Christ, the perfect judge will be our judge. We will be saved by grace, and judged of our works. If we have done something wrong in this world, we can use Jesus Christ name to ask our Heavenly Fathers forgiveness. Because Jesus died for our sins, we can be forgiven. When Jesus is judging us he will assign us to one of three kingdoms. He taught us that the three kingdoms differ like the sky. One kingdom is represented by the stars, the Telestial kingdom, which is the lowest of all the glories. The next best kingdom is the represented by the moon, which is the Terrestrial kingdom, which is the middle glory. The highest kingdom, where Heavenly Father and Jesus Christ live is the Celestial Kingdom. If we live the gospel, repent of our sins, and do all that we can in this life, the Lord has promised that there is place reserved for us there. In the Celestial Kingdom, Jesus taught that there are many mansions (super big castle houses) and we can have one of our own there. I hope we can all live there together some day. Heavenly Father is awesome, isn't he?

The rest of the hour is spent watching for shooting stars and finding patterns and designs that look like animals and shapes. It is a lot of fun. Please notice that this lesson does not end with a, "in the name of Jesus Christ, Amen." Our teachings of the Plan of Salvation should be casual and natural, and do not need to be formal. The formality of the traditional pronouncement can get in the way of the teaching, so I don't use it here, but please do as the spirit dictates to you.

Doctrine and Covenants 76: 96-98
"And the glory of the celestial is one, even as the glory of the sun is one. And the glory of the terrestrial is one, even as the glory of the moon is one. And the glory of the telestial is one, even as the glory of the stars is one; for as one star differs from another star in glory, even so differs one from another in glory in the telestial world."

PREPARATION:
- ✓ Pray and study your scriptures and ask the Lord to bless you as you seek to connect your son to his gospel.
- ✓ Fast the Sunday before ManCamp asking for the Lord's blessing.
- ✓ Research the stars above. See Spiritual Lessons - The Ant
- ✓ Check the website www.raisingboysintomen.com to see if there are any videos you may need to watch to prepare.
- ✓ Invite mommy to say a prayer right before you leave for ManCamp, asking Heavenly Father to keep her boys in safety.

CHALLENGE:
- ✓ Set a deer trap
- ✓ Construct a Survival Fire & Light the Fire with Flint and Steel
- ✓ Locate a Safe Drinking Water Source(s), build a water purifier.
- ✓ Reaffirm the invitation for him to set a goal to one day hold the Aaronic priesthood, and to read his scriptures daily

REWARD:
- ✓ A hatchet

JOURNAL:
- ✓ Mental – How can I do better in my subjects at school? How will doing my best now help me later in life?
- ✓ Physical – How can participating in sports on teams and staying active set me up for an active lifestyle when I am an older person?
- ✓ Spiritual – What does it mean, Jesus died for my sins?
- ✓ Fun - My favorite thing that happened at ManCamp was…
- ✓ Photo Page

NOTES:

Safe Drinking Water

In a survival situation, clean drinking water is a top priority. Teach your son to locate a fresh quick-moving stream. Show him the difference between standing and quickly moving water in a water bottle. A stream is ideal, but sometimes a slew is the only source available.

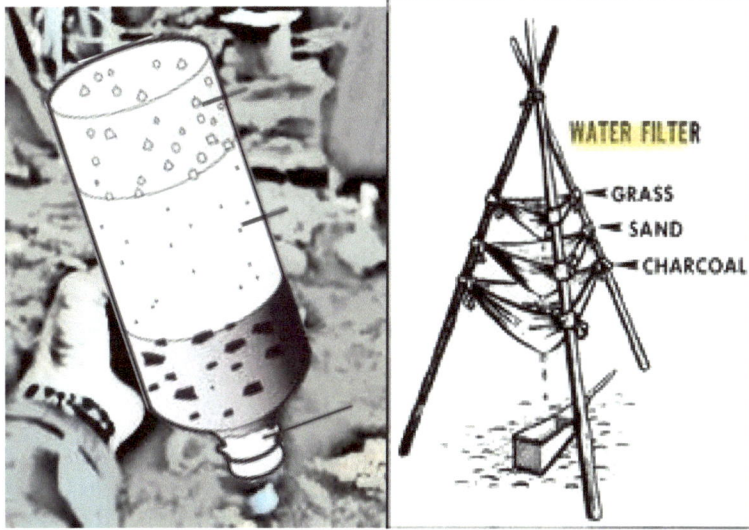

WATER FILTER
GRASS
SAND
CHARCOAL

While your son is constructing his survival fire, take the opportunity to construct a water purifier (Always use water tabs, or other water, while camping, but this is good to know if you were in a survival situation). He will use yours as an example. Take a 1L (think big) plastic water bottle and cut the very bottom off of it. Next take some medium sized rocks (handful about 1.5" in diameter) and put them into the bottle. If they are too small they will come out the drinking hole. Create layers as follows, two handfuls of natural grass, 2 handfuls of small rocks (sand), and 3 handfuls of ashes. Repeat until you reach the top of the water bottle, ending with small rocks. As you dump water through your filter, it will reduce the amount of skuz in the water, and if you run water through it a few times, each time it will pull more skuz from it. It is not going to be clean, but it beats the pond water, and will eliminate a lot of contaminants, and reduce the odds of getting sick. As I said before, do not really drink this water, only drink water you know is potable, but this is a skill worth having in a survival situation. Now let him build one.

Deer Trap

(Prior to building this trap, please view my online video tutorial. Go to www.raisingboysintomen.com)

Setting a deer trap is very difficult, and because the tree that is bent for the spring is large, your son will need your support. Resist the urge to "help." You are able to instruct the entire time, but what would it teach him if you were to take over? Your son can do this! Let him know that he has all day if he needs it, and remind him that it is not a race, and there is no pressure. This trap is way more advanced, and you could remind him that if he were truly in a survival situation, he would need to keep his cool, and focus on the task at hand.

Deer Tracks

Use Deer Tracks to Determine
What Type of Deer You are Tracking

Size		Type
1-1/2 in.		Fawn
2 in.		Yearling Doe
2 -1/2 in.		Adult Doe or Yearling Buck
3 in.		2-1/2 Year Old Buck
3-1/2 - 4 in.		3-1/2 Year Old & Older Bucks

Providing for oneself can be done catching squirrels, but to provide for a

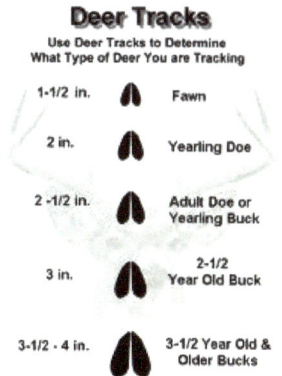

family one must be substantially more prepared. A 9-year old boy (believe it or not) is strong enough and capable enough to be the Man of any household, and when he masters what is required of him this year at ManCamp, he will have the self-confidence to believe in himself.

This year, setting a deer trap will give him the ability to acquire a sufficient quantity of meat to provide for a family for substantial period of time. You will need 50' of rope, a pocket knife and two medium length nails. This trap functions in a very similar fashion to the rabbit trap, and if you have mastered that trap, this trap is only slightly more difficult. The trap relies on the stored kinetic energy of a bent sapling tree. Find a game trail, and teach your son to look for deer tracks and tracks of other animals. It is similar to the rabbit trap, but instead of two pieces of wood notched together, the tension is applied to a trigger stick, and a larger tree is used for the stored energy. Due to its complexity, a more detailed description can be found in the video section of my website. Please watch the how-to video posted on my website prior to attempting this trap. The deer trap is one of the most difficult traps to set, so don't let your son get discouraged.

Lighting a Fire with Flint and Steel

Lighting a fire with flint and steel is very difficult, unless you have the sharp edge of a knife striking with the perfect stroke. If your son is in jeans, he could always lightly shave some of the jeans away near his foot. A sharp blade can shave a small puff of cotton without too much wear on his clothing, and it catches a spark. It will likely take him a few dozen tries before he is remotely close to getting it correct, let him struggle, but do not do it for him! You could also have handy the survival bracelet. If you soak the rope in a pan of melted paraffin wax it creates a highly flammable combination, also, your survival bracelets could contain a strand of jute. Encourage him, and express your confidence in his abilities.

Priesthood Discussion

Now is a great time to speak with your son about the importance of holding the Holy Priesthood. It might be good to review the qualifications of a deacon, and what he needs to prepare. The laying on of hands is the procedure revealed by the Lord to perform some of his most sacred ordinances. It allows for the blessing and healing of the sick, the confirmation of the Holy Spirit following baptism, the ordination to priesthood offices, and the setting-apart for callings within the church. It allows for priesthood blessings given by fathers, and for patriarchal blessings bestowed when individuals feel ready. In using the Priesthood, we are able to do the Lord's work, with His authority.

Spiritual Lessons
The Ant

Get a deep plastic cup and write the word, "SIN" on it with a sharpie, but don't let your son see that side of the cup until it is time to teach him. Find and ant hill, preferably black ants as they do not bite like their red cousins. Take an ant and place it somewhere that you will be able to watch it for a while (like a gravel road or a beach). Ask you son if he could construct something that could stop the ant, without killing it or trapping it? Maybe he could create an ant maze of some sort. Point out to your son as you watch the ant work that he will notice that the ant is not deterred by any obstacle. After you have messed with the ant for a while, capture the ant in the cup. Tell your son that so far the only obstacle that you have been able to find that can deter an ant is a glass cup that has a 90 degree incline, and a plastic cup. As you watch it struggle, you can explain that being capture in the cup is like being captured in a sin that can't be beaten. Reveal the word "SIN" on the cup. If any creature that God has created can get itself out of a predicament it is the ant, and even the ant is defeated by the cup. After you watch it struggle for a while, ask your son how you could rescue the ant from sin? He will probably say, "dump the cup," or "put a stick in that it can climb," or "add grass until it can climb out." Ask your son, "can the ant do it alone, without our help?" He might have some creative ideas, but remind him that he can't get out of the cup no matter how hard he tries. Have your son lower the stick for the ant to climb, let your son know that he is saving the ant, just like the Savior Jesus Christ saves us. Jesus can save us no matter what sin we find ourselves in. We need to always call on the name of Jesus Christ to rescue us from the pitfall of sin, and just like we saved the ant, Jesus will always save us.

Helaman 5:12

"And now, my sons, remember, remember that it is upon the rock of our Redeemer, who is Christ, the Son of God, that ye must build your foundation; that when the devil shall send forth his mighty winds, yea, his shafts in the whirlwind, yea, when all his hail and his mighty storm shall beat upon you, it shall have no power over you to drag you down to the gulf of misery and endless wo, because of the rock upon which ye are built, which is a sure foundation, a foundation whereon if men build they cannot fall."

39

PREPARATION:
- ✓ Pray and study your scriptures and ask the Lord to bless you as you seek to connect your son to his gospel.
- ✓ Fast the Sunday before ManCamp asking for the Lord's blessing.
- ✓ Research the story about Captain Moroni and how he raised the Standard of Liberty as found in Alma 46-48
- ✓ See Spiritual Lessons – The Super Hero-Captain Moroni, and The Family Standard of Liberty at the Pinnacle of the Mountain.
- ✓ Check the website www.raisingboysintomen.com to see if there are any videos you may need to watch to prepare.
- ✓ Invite mommy to say a prayer right before you leave for ManCamp, asking Heavenly Father to keep her boys in safety.

CHALLENGE:
- ✓ Assemble a shelter (dad helps gather materials)
- ✓ Set a deer trap.

REWARD:
- ✓ A survival knife.

JOURNAL:
- ✓ Mental – What does it mean to do your best in school, and to read good books?
- ✓ Physical – Taking care of your physical Body is important, what does it mean to get the proper rest, relaxation, diet and exercise?
- ✓ Spiritual – How can choosing to obey the commandments help you life a better life? How can you tell Heavenly Father loves you?
- ✓ Fun - My favorite thing that happened at ManCamp was…
- ✓ Photo Page

NOTES:

Create a Shelter

Your son will create a lean-to shelter patterned after the picture below. Smaller people should construct a smaller shelter; it will result in less heat loss later. Find a long (10') or so relatively straight pole from the deadfall, and remove any branches. This will be your main cross beam. Next locate two sticks approximately 8 inches in diameter and about 6 feet in length. Using 5' of rope, latchet the logs together about 6" from the ends in a V pattern. This will be the opening to the shelter pictured below. Lay the cross-beam onto the upside-down V, and latchet it to the V, and you have the basic skeleton. Now lay solid branches against the skeleton. Next gather branches and weave them in and out between the branches in a large patchwork. The more branches, the less rain will penetrate, and the less draft. For this step you will need green branches, as they are less flammable. You could also cut natural grass (sort of like sod for your house, only natures version) and lay that on the shelter as well. Next have your son gather dry grass from the area and place it on the floor of the lean-to. Pine needles are also good, but they are flammable, and they are pokey when it comes time to sleep.

The Super Hero – Captain Moroni

(Alma 43-44, Alma 48:10-17)

As you hike, locate a ravine with a river or stream flowing through it. It is preferable if the incline is relatively steep on both sides if you can find such a place, but that is not required. Find a rock to stop and have a snack and water break. Throwing a few stones in the stream can be fun while you start your short spiritual message. Ask your son, "who is your favorite super hero?" When he responds, ask him, "what do you admire about that hero? Is it the X-ray vision, the ability to fly, or _____ (sub in the appropriate attribute)?" Let your son tell you about the attribute and how it works. Let him know that you think that hero is really cool too, but remind him that that hero is fictitious (not real). This is a great time to introduce your hero to him. You could say, "Do you know who my real life hero is?" Let him answer affirmatively. "My favorite hero is found in the Book of Mormon, his name was Captain Moroni, he was a military leader who was so crafty and righteous that the meanest bad guys in the world feared him, even Satan is afraid of him. He is so awesome that before Satan goes to bed at night he looks under his bed for Captain Moroni before he feels safe (if he is older he will probably get the joke, if not, that is ok too). Let me tell you about him. Captain Moroni was a great military leader who lived about 80 B.C. He was not only powerful with the sword, and in command of the military he was also a man of strong faith in the Lord. It was said of Moroni that if all men were like him the very powers of hell would have been shaken forever, and the devil would not be able to lead us astray. He was spying on the movement of the other army gathering information, but what was super sneaky, he went to the Lord's prophet, and asked him what they should do. The prophet told Moroni where to set his armies, pretty cool huh? The army he was facing was very large, in fact they were greatly outnumbered. Captain Moroni hid a part of his army on the far side of the river on the high ground." Point to the ridge above where you are sitting. "They hid there (pointing) by laying down so the enemy army could not see them. They hid all along the ridge all the way up and down so there was nowhere for the enemy army to get through. Then Captain Moroni waited for the Lamanites to pass by his army toward the river. Once they were past Captain Moroni ordered his army to attack with all their might to drive the Lamanites toward the river. The enemy army had given up the high ground, and chose to run toward the river to escape. The other side would allow them to regain the high ground against the army attacking them on the rear. As the large army of the Lamanites got across the river Captain Moroni ordered his men on the other side to attack. At that point the Lamanites were completely surrounded, disorganized, and losing soldiers by the hundreds. For the army of Captain Moroni, it was like shooting at fish in a barrel. As Captain Moroni saw the confusion of his enemies, he ordered his men to take several steps back, and to stop killing the Lamanites. Captain Moroni gave the surviving Lamanites the option to throw down their weapons and promise to never return to war against them, and they would let them go. If they would not make the promise, never to return to war, he gave them back their weapons and ordered his men back to battle. It shows how merciful, and how he didn't really want to hurt anyone. Captain Moroni was a peaceful man. Captain Moroni's army won, and eventually all the enemies made the promise, or were killed. Pretty awesome story if you ask me. That is why he is my hero, he wanted peace so bad he was willing to go to war to get it. He was merciful even to a terrible enemy. He was righteous and followed the prophet, he was a faithful man to the Lord. I hope one day I can be as awesome as Captain Moroni, and I know you are already on that path. I am very proud of you, you are a good boy, and one day you will be a great man, like Captain Moroni." Now I start to pack my snack and water, and get ready to hike some more.

Family Standard of Liberty at the Pinnacle of the Mountain
(Alma 46, Alma 48:10-17)

You will need a pocket knife (or a sharpie marker), and a stick about 5 inches in diameter. As you reach the top of a large hike, it is great to relax. I like to locate a stick and carve a message into it quickly. It is very meaningful if you ask your son what you should carve in case someone 100 years from now finds the stick. He might say something like, "Hamilton Boys, Hiked Here 2013," or something like that. Guide the carving ideas to something spiritual as you are making suggestions. I might carve something like, "Hamilton Boys, Serve God Forever 2013!" When I am done, I have my son pound the stick into the ground. While he does that I tell him how awesome it is, what we just did. I compliment him for being such a good boy, and how proud I am of him. Then I crack out some trail mix and a special yummy snack that I had hidden. I recommend granola bars covered in chocolate, but any yummy snack will work. I start by saying something like, "remember Captain Moroni, they guy I told you about. He used to do something like we just did. He was a righteous man, and he saw great wickedness in his city. He saw all the people sinning, and not remembering Heavenly Father. Worse yet, there was a man in the land named Amalickiah who had gained great power in the government and was seeking to overthrow the liberty and freedom of the people. Worse even yet, he was a wicked man who was teaching everyone to sin. One day, Captain Moroni knelt on the ground and prayed for Heavenly Father to bless him. He then tore his coat and created a flag, something I call the standard of liberty. Just like how we just wrote our message his message was even cooler. He wrote, 'In memory of our God, our religion, and freedom, and our peace, our wives and our children." Moroni walked up the street carrying this banner and formed an army. He marched to parts of the land that were wicked, and he caused everyone to fly his standard of liberty flag or be killed. He compelled them to hoist the standard of liberty everywhere he went as a token of their commitment to uphold freedom in the country. Eventually Amalickiah ran away with a few of his men like a coward, and for a short time, peace and liberty was again restored to the land of the Nephites, because of what Captain Moroni did. He is a great example of standing up for what is right. For a while it was just him, and the Lord of course, but that must have taken real courage. Moroni could have just given in to wickedness, and Amalickiah would have probably given him a lot of money to stay out of the way. Captain Moroni could have just gone along with the wickedness in the land. That is a really good lesson for us. Sometimes we have to stand up for what is right, and by doing that, sometimes we may need to stand alone. But we are never really alone, God will always be by our side when we are doing what is right. We can be like Captain Moroni by sticking up for a kid who is getting picked on at school. We can be like Captain Moroni when we choose to say "no" to the temptations of this world. We can say "no" to cigarettes, alcohol, naked pictures, and saying bad words. We can be just like Captain Moroni when we exercise courage to do what Heavenly Father has asked us to do. I am working hard to be like Captain Moroni, and I have seen you already making really good choices. I believe one day you can be just like Captain Moroni and it will be said of you, the very jaws of hell are shaken, and the devil checks under his bed for you. Heavenly Father will help you, if you will let him. Pretty cool huh?" About now I pat my son on the back, and ask him if he thinks archeologists will dig up our stick one day and know what we believe in and laugh. Throwing some rocks or sticks is a good time before it is time to head back. Well done dad! Even Captain Moroni would be proud of the dad you are at this point!

The Prophet Joseph Smith
"The Standard of Truth has been erected; no unhallowed hand can stop the work from progressing; persecutions may rage, mobs may combine, armies may assemble, calumny may defame, but the truth of God will go forth boldly, nobly, and independent, till it has penetrated every continent, visited every clime, swept every country, and sounded in every ear, till the purposes of God shall be accomplished, and the Great Jehovah shall say the work is done."

PREPARATION:
- ✓ Pray and study your scriptures and ask the Lord to bless you as you seek to connect your son to his gospel.
- ✓ Fast the Sunday before ManCamp asking for the Lord's blessing.
- ✓ Research and know the components of the Armour of God.
- ✓ See Spiritual Lessons – Armour of God and Daughters of God.
- ✓ Check the website www.raisingboysintomen.com to see if there are any videos you may need to watch to prepare.
- ✓ Invite mommy to say a prayer right before you leave for ManCamp, asking Heavenly Father to keep her boys in safety.

CHALLENGE:
- ✓ Build a shelter
- ✓ Create a Heat Deflection Rock Wall outside of the Shelter
- ✓ Build a deer trap
- ✓ Build and Light a Survival Fire with Flint and Steel
- ✓ Learn basic flint napping skills and create a water filtration system.
- ✓ Read and create Topographical Maps.
- ✓ Invite him to gain his own testimony of Jesus Christ
- ✓ Optional: Place a time Capsule somewhere to be located in 10 -20 years.

REWARD:
- ✓ A Bow and Arrows.

JOURNAL:
- ✓ Mental – How does studying for tests and quizzes help me do better?
- ✓ Physical – What fitness goals could I start making for myself? By this time next year, could I do 30-30-30 in 3 minutes or less? (30 Push-ups, 30 Sit-ups, 30 Jumping-Jacks) Set a goal for this coming year.
- ✓ Spiritual –How does my example affect others perceptions about my Master Jesus Christ? This year I will turn 12 and be ready to receive the Aaronic Priesthood, what can I do to be prepared to perform that duty?
- ✓ Fun - My favorite thing that happened at ManCamp was…
- ✓ Photo Page

NOTES:

Independence

As you may have already noticed, each year is successively harder, and each year builds on the previous year. This year, your son will learn all the necessary skills for comprehensive survival. This is the year of his true independence! As rough as it may be to watch him do so much work, you must let him do it, as accomplishing large tasks is a part of his growth. Believe it or not, this is the year your son has the opportunity to become a man. My sons walk confidently and your son will too. Do not let him give up, but break each task into pieces if he needs it, and you can act as a coach every step of the way. Ask him if he remembers what to do in each case. Coach him with questions, be the cheerleader and water boy, but DO NOT do it for him. Continue to speak kind encouraging words, remind him how impressed you are of his work, and let him know that you think he is doing well. You can scout good materials, you can give him ideas, you can remind him to take breaks every 20 minutes to think and reassess where he is headed in the project, but as a reminder, do not do it for him. The year a boy crosses over to becoming a man is a big year, and his confidence will be forever unshaken if you can see him through this year!

Deer Trap

Setting a deer trap, like he did last year, and building a deer trap are two very different endeavors. Once your son builds, sets, and tests his deer trap, and sees that it works, it will give him a huge boost of confidence! Be sure to congratulate him often, as this trap could provide enough meat for an entire family for weeks! In reality, the trap is very basic, and you would need to set a few dozen traps, in a highly populated deer area to catch one. Please do not leave this trap armed unattended, unless you are in a real survival situation. If you trap a deer in this trap, you will need to either have a firearm to finish the job, or one massively long spear to finish the job. A panicked deer is extremely dangerous! In a survival situation, this trap, and others like it should be checked periodically to ensure an animal is not suffering! If you catch it, you have to eat it, so don't trap it if you don't have the guts to put the animal down and eat it.

Heat Deflector

Preparing a heat deflector is very important to heat conservation. It can significantly increase the heat retention your fire may offer by deflecting heat back toward the entrance to your lean-to. It is especially important if you are surviving in sub-zero temperatures, and this one small trick could save your life. Approximately 2-3' from the entrance dig a shallow hole 6" deep 2' x 2'. Pile the dirt on the far side of the hole away from the entrance. Next, stack rocks about 3 feet high with the rock faces aimed toward the entrance of the lean-to, as this will help deflect additional heat from the survival fire into the lean-to. This deflector can also be made using logs angled properly, but, if you have the time, rocks are superior, although the wood could be used as emergency burn supply, so it is a trade- off.

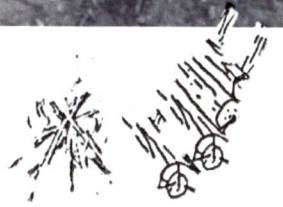

Flint Napping

Flint napping dates back to prehistoric man in technique, and may actually be one of the technologies that allowed man to fight the sabre tooth, rather than run from one. With that aside, flint napping has become a modern art, with various developed styles and techniques. This volume will focus on the basics. Locate a stone that is elongated in shape, smooth on all surfaces, and that can be tightly gripped, based on the size of your hand. This will serve as your striker stone.

Next, gather approximately 10 rocks that are roughly the size of two of your fists put together. Believe it or not, most stones will work fine, but the very best ones will look like a big piece of glass! The Aztecs used Obsidian shards on their weapons which were extremely black and shiny, and also, as sharp as a razor blade. If your camp area has nothing that looks like an old beer bottle colored rock, you can use a bunch of riverbed rocks. (A beer bottle would actually work as well, but that has too much risk of getting glass in the eyes for beginners, so I do not advise that). Wear eye protection, stretch out your limbs thoroughly, wear pants that overlap the top of your shoes, sit comfortably, and place a doubled over towel on your leg just above the knee, this will be your work area. In your dominant hand take the striker stone, and in the other hand take one of your glassy-looking rocks. Hold the glassy-looking rock against your leg above the knee area a few inches on the inside of your leg on the towel. In a forceful direct downward motion strike the glassy-colored stone with the striker stone rounded blunt end. If you have hit it correctly, you will have broken the glassy colored stone, repeat this until you get the feel of the striking motion. Over the next half hour, you will develop better angles for striking, and you will get the hang of flint napping. It is not rocket science, it has been done for thousands of years, but preparing the perfect arrowhead is truly an art form. Remember, ugly and sharp kills an animal just as easily as pretty and sharp, so don't be discouraged if your work product is not as great as you think it should be. You will eventually discover ways to get sharp edges from the rocks, be patient. Attempt to refine some of your edges. Do you see how the natives on the plains mastered the arrow tip? Create an arrowhead, and put it on an arrow. Find a loose thread on your old camping blanket and pull it out. This will be a great way to tie on your arrowhead. You can also use floss or thread, or twine, or damp animal leather. (TIP: It will dull a knife quickly, but a knife can be a useful tool to fine tune a flint knapped rock) Above all, BE PATIENT! You will try 1,000 before one is even close to one the natives used.

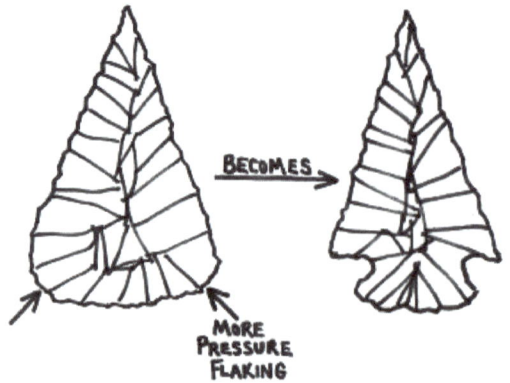

BECOMES

MORE PRESSURE FLAKING

Bow Basics

Stance should be comfortable, solid, about shoulder width apart with the front foot slightly angled toward the target.

Place your arrow in ready position with the odd colored feather facing upward when your arrow is nocked.

Make a finger pistol using your off hand forefinger and thumb. Point it at the target, now turn it 90" so your palm is facing the ground. This is how your hand should look when you finally grip the bow. Not attempt to grip the bow in your off hand at the joint of the pad where your thumb and forefinger meet. If you shoot an arrow and do this step incorrectly, your whole forearm will get whipped from the bowstring on its way to deliver the arrow.

Take a few deep breaths.

If you have a release, place it on your draw loop, if you do not, use your forefinger and middle finger at the first joint and place one above and one below the nock on the string.

Shooting a Bow

Draw your arrow keeping it pointed down range at all times! Attempt to anchor your shooting hand to the same place each shot, usually the jaw area. Always wear an arm guard to protect your arm from getting bow string slapped.

Time Capsule

If you decided to place a time capsule, this is a good year to do it. Contents might include a letter to yourself, a letter to your son. It could include you sons toy, some photos etc. You could take the time to draw a small treasure map in the back of your sons ManCamp Journal. If you feel ambitious, you could attempt a typographical map with X marking the spot. Be sure to record details in the exact location, like big unmovable rocks. Avoid things like trees, or paths. Have fun, be creative! PVC piping with glued caps make nice ones, or you can view my website if you would like to purchase one.

Topographical Mapping

Basic topographical mapping attempts to view various landforms and altitude levels from a birds eye approach. The tighter the lines are together, the steeper the incline. Practice a few times, and you could have your son attempt one for himself. (Please view my website video for more explanation and detail.)

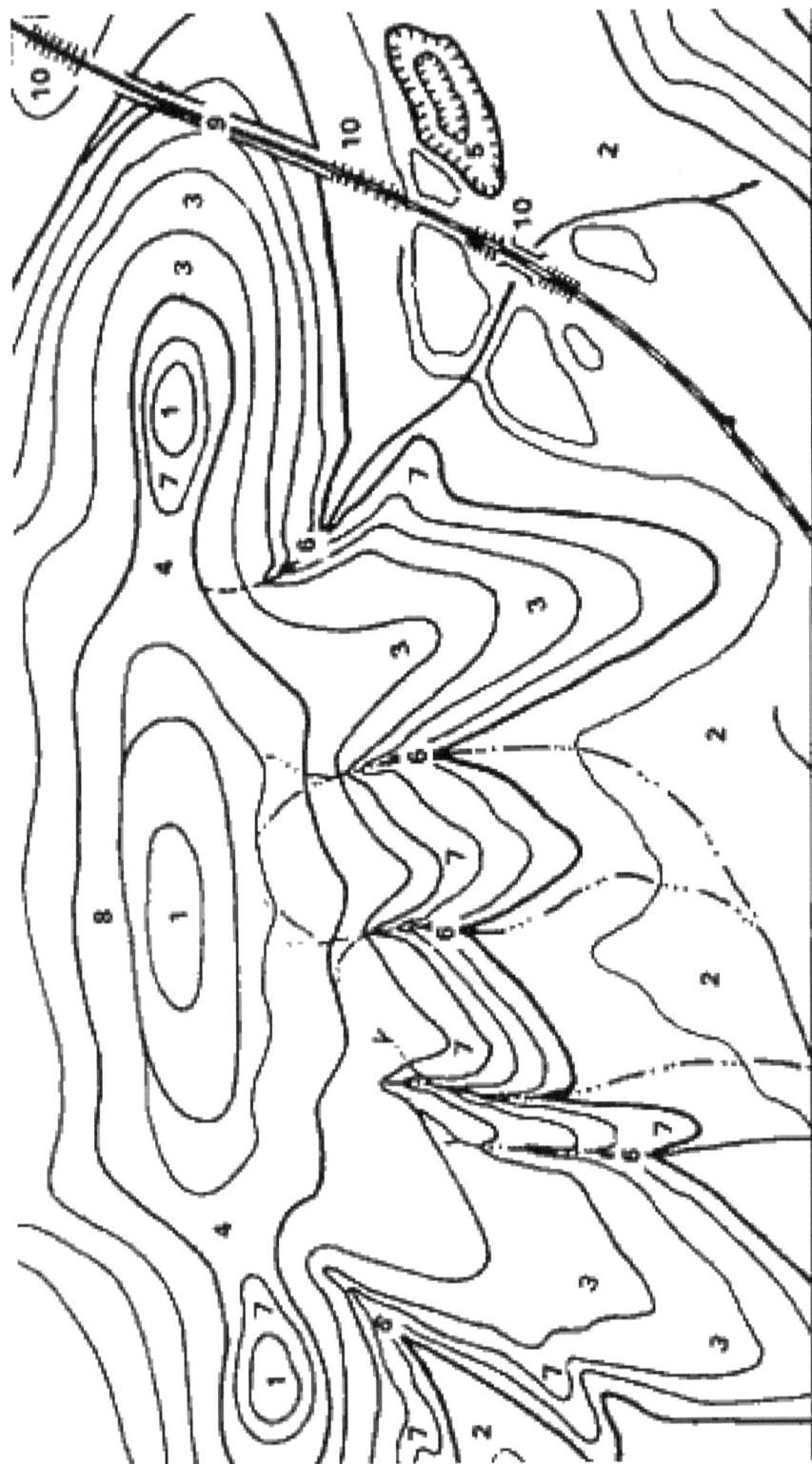

1. HILL   3. RIDGE   5. DEPRESSION   7. SPUR   9. CUT

2. VALLEY   4. SADDLE   6. DRAW   8. CLIFF   10. FILL

Spiritual Lessons
The Armor of God
On your hike, or while sitting by the campfire, start talking with your son, when the feeling or timing is right. You can take a break on your hike by sitting down and cracking out the trail mix.

Say, "The battle lines are drawn. There is no neutral ground."

Get a stick and write in the dirt, (Lord / Satan).

Ask your son, "Which side do you choose?" If he chooses Satan, all hope is not lost, you just have to say, "Ok, but that is the side where you will lose," but that selection is highly unlikely if you have taught him the gospel. When he says, "the Lords side," ask him if he knows "that that side always wins?" When he answers, jump to the side that says Satan with a stick and say, "Enguard" or whatever they say in the movies before a sword fight, and put on a huge smile. Your son will quickly find a stick to defend himself. As we sword fight for a couple of minutes, I let him defeat me, just as I am about to win. Be sure not to hurt him, as this will be a bad lesson, and if you end up getting hurt, learn to sword fight better, you should be able to beat a boy.

When the fighting is over I like to sit and get a drink, and crack out a snack of trail mix. Now is the time for teaching. Start by saying, "the weapons and preparations that you are making right now will help you, you know? I was asking what kinds of things you would take to war, but the war is already underway. The book of Mormon had a war like the one I described."

Get a stick and draw the battle on the ground as you tell the story.

Say, "Terrible and wicked Lamanites were invading the Nephite land, and just when the battle was about to be lost, a group of young men enlisted in the military. They weren't old at all, some just a few years older than you. It was said that because of their great faith, they could not be destroyed in battle. They entered into a covenant with God that they would fight for the liberty of the Nephites, and lay down their lives if necessary in defense of liberty. The scriptures describe the boys as exceedingly valiant for courage, they were strong and full of energy, kind of like you. Above all, it is said, they were men who were true at all times in whatsoever thing they were entrusted. They were taught to keep the commandments of God from a young age. Their faith was strong in the Lord.

One day, Captain Antipus and Helaman devised a plan to lure the Lamanites out to battle. They loaded the boys up with baskets of grain and bananas and marched them on a trail near a city occupied by a strong Lamanite Army.

The Lamanites figured they could kill the little boys, and so they left the safety of the city to chase them. The boys waited until the army of the Lamanites was right behind them, then they dropped the baskets of bananas and started to run. The Lamanites saw them run and wanted to kill them, so they started chasing them." The boys ran for several hours eventually down a small valley and out the other side.

The army of Antipus hid on the sides of the valley and waited for the Army of the Lamanites to pass them by, thereby cutting off their ability to retreat. When the army passed them by, they began to attack them on

49

the rear so fiercely that the army of the Lamanites had to turn around and face them. That is why the Lamanites stopped chasing the boys. When Helaman saw that they were no longer being pursued he asked his boys what they thought they should do. Helaman asked his boys if they would turn and fight the entire Lamanite army. Helaman said of their response, "never had I seen so great a courage among all the Nephites, for they remembered the words of their mother's, that if they always kept the commandments of God, they would be protected." Helaman did not know if Antipus had caught the army, or if they were marching into a trap of the Lamanites, but as they arrived at the battlefield he discovered Antipus's army was beginning to lose because they had marched for so long that they were exhausted. The Lamanites were taking courage and beginning to break through the battle lines of Antipus's army when 2000 of the most ferocious warriors began killing them by the hundreds on the rear. In fact, the 2000 boys were so lethal, the entire army turned to fight them. That gave Antipus's men enough time to regroup, rest, and return to battle. Now the Lamanites were surrounded, and they eventually were killed, but some of the army surrendered and were taken prisoner. Pretty cool story huh?"

Say, "Deciding on what side to fight for in a world full of filth can be tough. The Lord has instructed us to put on his armour. If you were going into battle, "Would you take a weapon?" "What do you think you could wear to protect your body?" "What would you wear on your feet?" "What would you need to protect yourself from arrows and a swinging sword?"

The Lord told us what the parts of His armour are. Just as Helaman and the 2000 young men had an enemy, you too have an enemy bent on your destruction. The war might not be with a real swords and shields but the writers of the scriptures (Paul) told us about our time, and what weapons we need. Our weapons are spiritual weapons. He told us that the things we need are Truth (probably avoid the loins part, as this will lead to a tangent, and an explanation about underwear, and can quickly digress to SpongeBob), and the breastplate of righteousness. This means we need to keep our heart strong and loyal to Heavenly Father. By keeping his commandments we show that we are loyal to him in our hearts. He said we need to have our feet shod in preparation of the gospel. This means that we need to learn, even at a young age, the value of standing up for what is right, and that we defend the Lords gospel in all things, and that we have learned the truth

The Armour of God

Loins girt about with Truth

Breastplate of Righteousness

Feet Shod with the Preparation of the Gospel of Peace

Shield of Faith

Helmet of Salvation

and have a firm footing in gospel truths. Just like the 2000 who had a knowledge of the gospel as taught by their mothers, you too have been taught the gospel.

We need to have a Shield, which represents our faith. Satan will try to shoot arrows at us when we least expect it, and if we are comfortably and safely behind our shield, he will be unable to snipe us from afar. You see Satan does not want to face us with a sword. He is a coward and a weakling, and he will attempt to fire an arrow at you from the shadows. He will aim at your weak points, and attempt to take you down without actually facing you. You put on your shield when you read your scriptures and say your prayers. Doing that every day is a shield.

Wearing the Helmet of Salvation is also important. Our thoughts will ultimately direct our actions, and if we are focused on our eternal reward in heaven, we will find our helmet firmly intact. As you stay away from filth in magazines, on the internet, on TV. etc. you are kept safe, you're your thoughts can be pure.

Notice that all the items so far have limited offensive capabilities? That is because defense against a sneaky enemy is essential, but the Lord did not leave us weaponless.

The Lord has given us the Sword of the Spirit. The example we set by our words and actions is the best offensive weapon we have. Other, including ourselves, can be cut deeply by the truths the Spirit teaches. As we are faithful to the Lord, he will enhance our weapons and defenses. We must be vigilant in keeping our sword sharp by keeping the Spirit with us always. We must shore up our footing by learning his gospel continually, and we must keep his commandments to keep our shield of faith bright. We must keep our hearts and minds clean so as not to be caught without our armour.

Share your testimony. It might be something like, "I want you to know that Satan is real. He is continually hunting you. He lurks in the shadows like a coward to steal your soul. I want you to know that if you put on the Whole Armour of God, he will keep you safe. You are a soldier on God's army, and if you will prepare yourself you will be kept safe, and the Lord will make you one of his finest soldiers. You have it in you, I so testify in the sacred name of Jesus Christ, Amen."

Ephesians 6:11-17
11 Put on the whole armour of God, that ye may be able to stand against the wiles of the devil.
12 For we wrestle not against flesh and blood, but against principalities, against powers, against the rulers of the darkness of this world, against spiritual wickedness in high places.
13 Wherefore take unto you the whole armour of God, that ye may be able to withstand in the evil day, and having done all, to stand.
14 Stand therefore, having your loins girt about with truth, and having on the breastplate of righteousness;
15 And your feet shod with the preparation of the gospel of peace;
16 Above all, taking the shield of faith, wherewith ye shall be able to quench all the fiery darts of the wicked.
17 And take the helmet of salvation, and the sword of the Spirit, which is the word of God."

Lamanite
Army
20,000

Nephite
Army of
Antipus
8,000

Lamanite
Army
20,000

Helaman + 2,000
Boys + Supplies

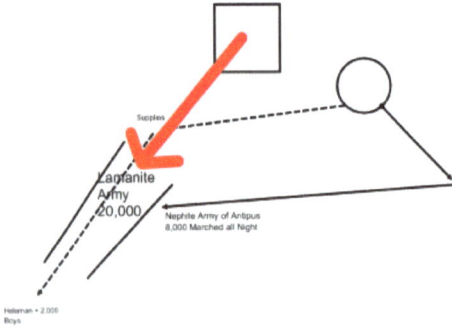

Nephite
Army of
Antipus
8,000

Supplies

Lamanite
Army
20,000

Nephite Army of Antipus
8,000 Marched all Night

Helaman + 2,000
Boys

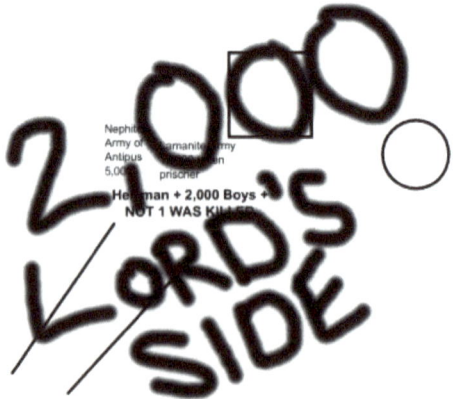

WAR

Lamanite
Army
20,000

Nephite
Army of
Antipus
8,000

Helaman + 2,000 Boys

WAR

Lamanite
Army
20,000

Nephite
Army of
Antipus
8,000

WAR

Helaman + 2,000 Boys

2,000

Nephite
Army of
Antipus
5,000

Lamanite Army
taken in
prisoner

Helaman + 2,000 Boys +
NOT 1 WAS KILLED

LORD'S
SIDE

Daughters of God

Begin by asking your son, "Is there anyone at school or at church that you can tell doesn't like you." If your son indicates someone, let him expound who that person is. Ask your son, "How can you tell that person doesn't like you." Let him talk. Hopefully in his interactions he has noticed some verbal and nonverbal indicators of that person's distain for him. Ask him, "how would it make you feel if it was someone that you liked that treated you that way?'

Say, "Emotions can be a tough thing to manage, but we can manage more effectively how we treat others, especially girls. They have tender feelings, and like it or not, they sometimes have a lack of self-esteem. We should always be kind to all girls.

Girls should never fall victim to a disapproving glance or a harsh word. They deserve above all to feel sincere approval, from every man. Unfortunately, they do not always get what they deserve.

Consider two girls, one attractive, and the other, less-attractive, from a visual perspective. How do we interact with each of these young ladies? Should we show less kindness and friendliness to one over the other? Often the way individuals interact with others can be a tell-tale of who they are inside. A man who can dance and have fun equally with both ladies will find himself one day in love with a young lady who is beautiful inside and out. If we are unkind to one of these young ladies, the Lord can't be pleased. We should build daughters of God. Our words should only be positive, and we should seek to harness our thoughts so we can see all young ladies as the beautiful flower that they are, regardless of the color of their pedals or size of their bulb. They are God's creation, and we acquit or convict ourselves each time we choose to be kind or mean.

It is not just physical appearance that might affect how we treat someone. In St. Mathew 25:34-40, the Lord tells us, inasmuch as ye have done it unto one of these, the least of these my brethren, ye have done it unto me. Who are the least, as this scripture describes?" Let your son answer, and it might be a good opportunity for him to discover a few things about how he has been treating people, whether on purpose or not.

Testify. You might say, "Remember that the Lord, in His creation saved the best for last! We should always seek to build the self-esteem of every girl we encounter. The Lord will bless you, as you show kindness to all girls." At this point I usually give my son a nudge and say, if you aren't nice, maybe none of them will go on a date with you.

PREPARATION:
- ✓ Pray and study your scriptures and ask the Lord to bless you as you seek to connect your son to his gospel.
- ✓ Fast the Sunday before ManCamp asking for the Lord's blessing.
- ✓ Research the function of how the human body heals.
- ✓ See Spiritual Lessons – Jesus Christ the Healer of Man's Soul and Daughters of God (see Age 11).
- ✓ Check the website www.raisingboysintomen.com to see if there are any videos you may need to watch to prepare.
- ✓ Invite mommy to say a prayer right before you leave for ManCamp, asking Heavenly Father to keep her boys in safety.

CHALLENGE:
- ✓ Identify ideal and safe places to camp
- ✓ Identify and recognize plants that are edible
- ✓ Spend one night alone in a tent
- ✓ Create a Spear
- ✓ Administer first aid to a cut or a burn (pretend-hopefully!)
- ✓ Invite him to set a goal to one day serve a full-time mission.

REWARD:
- ✓ A .22 caliber rifle.* Get a good one, he will have it FOREVER!

JOURNAL:
- ✓ Mental – How is school going? Each time there is an assignment am I prepared to take responsibility for myself to complete it on time? What goals do I have for my learning this year? How many books can I set a goal to read this year?
- ✓ Physical – Can I run 2 miles? How am I taking care of my body? What goals do I have for this year?
- ✓ Spiritual – the duties of a deacon are to 1) pass the sacrament, 2) watch over the church, 3) warn, expound, exhort, and teach, and invite all to come unto Christ, 4) assist the bishop with temporal things, 5) fellowship quorum members and other young men. Explain how you are doing on each of these duties, and set a goal to help you fulfill each of them. What example can we gain from the 2,000 Sons of Helaman? How would Heavenly Father feel about the way I have been treating girls and women?
- ✓ Fun - My favorite thing that happened at ManCamp was…
- ✓ Photo Page

NOTES:

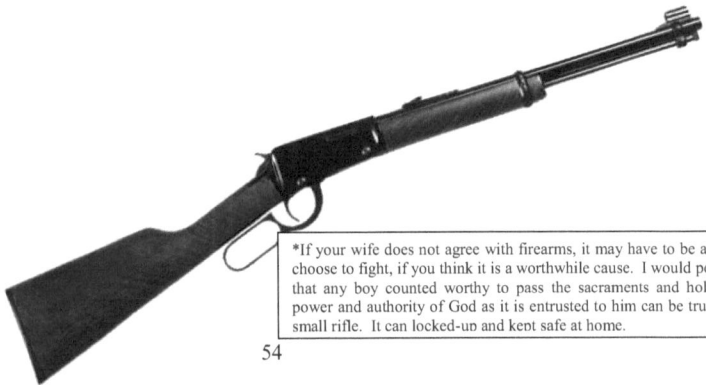

*If your wife does not agree with firearms, it may have to be a battle you choose to fight, if you think it is a worthwhile cause. I would petition you, that any boy counted worthy to pass the sacraments and hold the very power and authority of God as it is entrusted to him can be trusted with a small rifle. It can locked-up and kept safe at home.

Identify Edible Plants

Now that your son has the requisite skills to stay alive in the short-term, a few skills, cursory to immediate survival, are needed. The teachings begin to this year from a task oriented, accomplishment based system, to an overall approach to survival. Just as the army needs soldiers that can get tasks done, they also need officers to oversee the tasks to completion, and that is what the next few years are all about. Your son should have the self-confidence to attack any problems that life may throw at him, and feel like he can conquer. A wise man once said, wars are not won or lost with bullets, but with logistics. What does that mean? It means planning and global thinking are skills that must now be developed.

This year your son will learn to identify plants and edibles that naturally grow. There are several volumes to choose from, but are some superior productions:

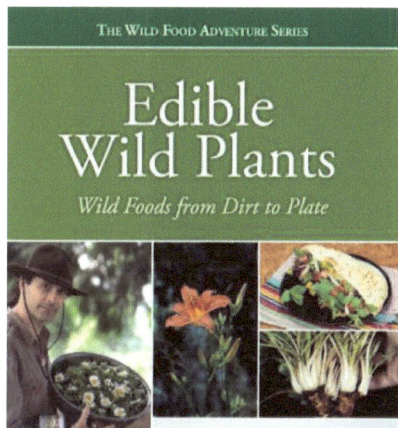

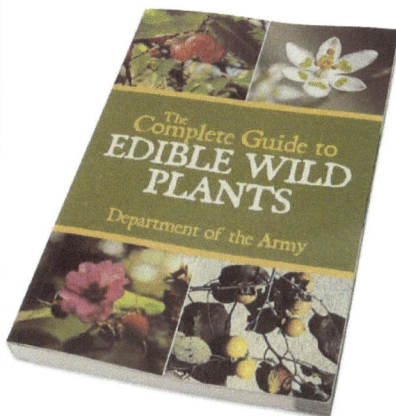

The Department of the Army book is good if you have a relatively sound knowledge of edibles found in nature, but the first one (Edible Wild Plants by Dr. John Kallas) is probably the best when it comes to the beginner, as the photos are full color, and there are warnings for lookalike plants alongside the edibles. Try to plan a meal with edibles your son has identified and collected, if you dare. It will probably not be the most appetizing meal you have ever digested, but it will be a great learning experience. Please be sure to eat items that you are confident in identifying, and are assured of their safety. A bad mushroom could result in a trip to the ER, or worse yet, the grave!

Create a Spear or Knife

Last year your son learned basic flint knapping skills. This year, your son should create a couple of spears, arrow heads, and a self-made knife. The natives used stretched moist hides, but 440 paracord will be ok for your spears, or dental floss or fishing line Attempt to create a small knife, wrap paracord around it for a handle.

First Aid

Caring for an injury is essential. Accidents happen, and knowing how to treat injury can be a matter of life and death. This section should not be used as a comprehensive guide, and proper training should be sought, but this is a layman's attempt to simplify the basics. The weekend could easily be occupied with a St. John's Ambulance level training, but that would be overstepping the basics. Your son should know how to properly bandage a cut, perform a mouth sweep with abdominal thrusts to force items from the mouth and throat, stop a nose bleed, flush an eye, and administer a

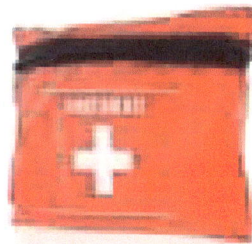

supportive tensile bandage to a joint. It may sound like a lot, but if you dedicate an hour, the basics can be covered. My eldest son choked, and I am thankful every day for the mouth sweep response I learned when I was a boy, it came natural, and it may have saved his life. Expensive supplies are not necessary; almost all the supplies can be found in your local dollar store.

Wounds/Cuts/Sprains
Clean the area if possible.
Remove clothes to better assess the wound and elevate the affected area.
Apply direct pressure (with a clean cloth if possible).
If bleeding does not stop, seek immediate medical attention.
For sprains wrap tensile bandage firm, but not tight, allow circulation.

Choking
DO NOT let the person out of your sight for several minutes!
Ask them to nod if they are choking – Yes or No.
Briskly pat them on the back between the shoulder blades.
Perform a mouth sweep.
Proceed to abdominal thrusts.
If item is dislodged, monitor the individual, in recovery position.
If immediate improvement does not show, call 911, and rush them to a medical facility!

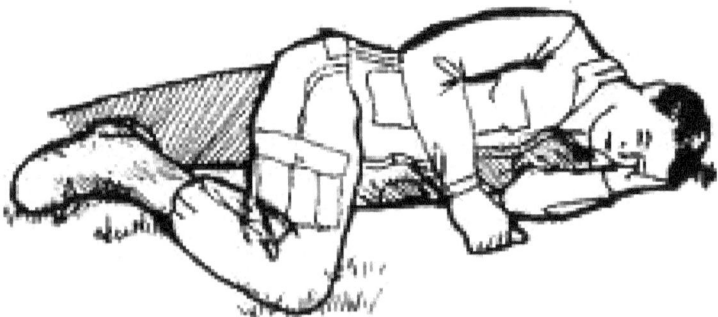

Abdominal Thrusts

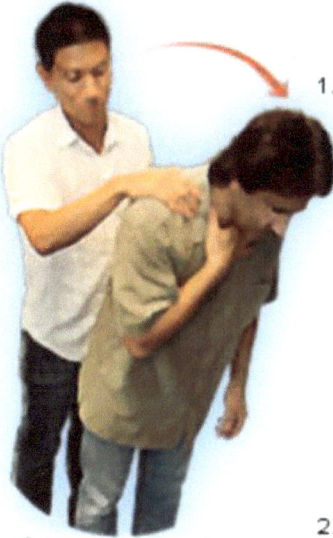

1. lean the person forward slightly and stand behind him or her.

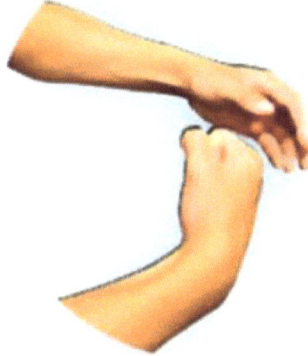

2. Make a fist with one hand.

3. Put your arms around the person and grasp your fist with your other hand near the top of the stomach, just below the center of the rib cage.

4. Make a quick, hard movement, inward and upward.

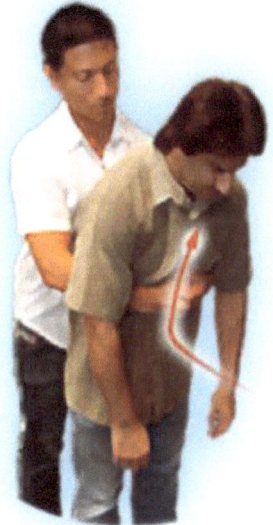

57

Nosebleeds

Lean forward.

Pinch nose at base of bone in nose on both sides.

Hold for 5 minutes, check, if bleeding continues, 10 minutes check.

If bleeding continues, you should seek medical attention.

If victim feels lightheaded, or if the nosebleed is as a result of severe head trauma (car accident or a football that did not hit the nose), seek immediate medical attention!

Do not blow nose for several hours, gently clean exterior with a damp cloth.

Image Credit: American Heart Association

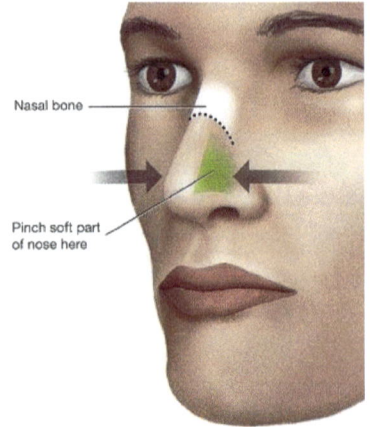

Nasal bone

Pinch soft part of nose here

Eyes Flushed

Encourage individual to tear and blink while facing down. Close eyes if necessary until debris collects near eyelid, and attempt to blink out.

Flush with water. Use a massive amount of water. When you think you are done, do it some more. 15-20 minutes is recommended.

15 Minutes▶

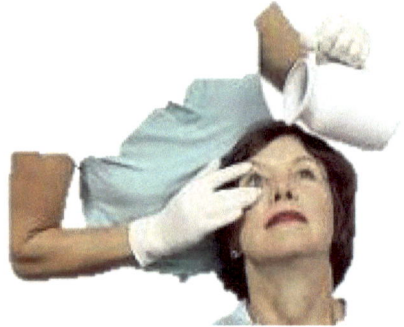

Spiritual Lessons
Jesus Christ the Healer of Man's Soul

As you are hiking, or sitting by the fire, tell your son, "I will do your best to keep you safe from people who would do him harm, and from any wild animal that would try to eat you. What would you do if a cougar jumped from the tree and tried to bite me?" Let your son answer. Use his answer to guide your response. If he says something like I would throw a rock at it, or I would hit it with a stick or I would shoot it with my BB gun build on it. Ask, "What would you do it a bad guy tried to take one of your friends when you are at baseball?" Let him answer. Hopefully you have taught him how to deal with situations like this.

Now transition the conversation with, "let me tell you a story about a time that some guys tried to grab Jesus. A gang of bad guys with torches heard Jesus was working on the Sabbath day, which was against the law at the time. They said he was an evil man who was trying to take over the government, and he was breaking all sorts of laws. They made up a lot of terrible lies up about him. When the mob of guys came to arrest him, Peter had a knife with him and just as they tried to grab Jesus, Peter whipped out his knife and cut a guy's ear. He sliced it really bad, and the mob looked on as the man crouched and screamed in agony. Just as there was about to be a large brawl, Jesus raised his voice and said, "Enough of this." Malchus (the member

58

of the mob) was bleeding as his ear had been cut really bad by Peter, so Jesus reached down and gave him an immediate priesthood blessing and commanded his ear to be healed. Pretty amazing isn't it?

Rather than fighting, Jesus let the mob arrest him. A short time later, they killed Jesus. I am always astounded at the example of Jesus. He was quick to heal and forgive rather than fight. He taught us to turn the other cheek when we are wronged. He returned good for evil and sought to heal rather than destroy.

Jesus was our perfect example. I love him, and I hope you can learn to love him even more. We show we love him when we keep his commandments. He is the Son of God, and I love Him. I hope you learn to heal others souls as he healed the man's ear. You can be an influence of healing in this world. If people are being unkind, you can be kind. If others are breaking the commandments, you can choose to follow the commandments. If others are bad, you can choose to be good.

Testify. "I know you are a boy of great integrity, I know that the Lord has a great many works in store for you. Be the Lord's healing hands. You are a fine boy, and I am thankful I have you. I hope you honor your priesthood, choose to serve a mission when it is time, and marry a fine young lady in the temple." I take the opportunity to pat him on the back, and after a moment of silence, I tell him, "the fire is getting low, can you throw on some wood?" Say, "have you thought of serving the Lord on a mission?" This is a great opportunity to talk about it with him, and see what you can do to help him. Listen to his concerns, and invite him to pray about it and set a goal to serve.

Matthew 14:14
14 And Jesus went forth, and saw a great multitude, and was moved with compassion toward them, and he healed their sick.

Psalm 23
1 The Lord is my shepherd; I shall not want.
2 He maketh me to lie down in green pastures: he leadeth me beside the still waters.
3 He restoreth my soul: he leadeth me in the paths of righteousness for his name's sake.
4 Yea, though I walk through the valley of the shadow of death, I will fear no evil: for thou art with me; thy rod and thy staff they comfort me.
5 Thou preparest a table before me in the presence of mine enemies: thou annointest my head with oil; my cup runneth over.
6 Surely goodness and mercy shall follow me all the days of my life: and I will dwell in the house of the Lord forever.

Daughters of God
(See Age 11)

PREPARATION:
- ✓ Pray and study your scriptures and ask the Lord to bless you as you seek to connect your son to his gospel.
- ✓ Fast the Sunday before ManCamp asking for the Lord's blessing.
- ✓ Research the effect of running water over rocks over millions of years. Notice how smooth they become.
- ✓ See Spiritual Lessons – Poisoned by Degrees, The Beggar, and Treasure your Blessings
- ✓ Write 2 Letters as described below.
- ✓ Check the website www.raisingboysintomen.com to see if there are any videos you may need to watch to prepare.
- ✓ Invite mommy to say a prayer right before you leave for ManCamp, asking Heavenly Father to keep her boys in safety.

CHALLENGE:
- ✓ Select camp spot
- ✓ 3 day survival trial (it is really only a 2 day survival) with 2 cans of beans, tent, flashlight, sleeping bag, 10 matches and 1 gallon of water, and knife
- ✓ Learn to tie food and packs from trees to avoid bears
- ✓ Invite him to learn his duty in the priesthood and do it, and to reaffirm his goal to one day serve a full-time mission.

REWARD:
- ✓ A $100 Cabela's gift card.

JOURNAL:
- ✓ Mental – What is my best subjects and why? What subjects do I need to work harder in to be successful?
- ✓ Physical – Why does a clean healthy body show Heavenly Father I am thankful for the gift of my body? Have I been showering daily and keeping my appearance clean like a missionary?
- ✓ Spiritual – the duties of a deacon are to 1) pass the sacrament, 2) watch over the church, 3) warn, expound, exhort, and teach, and invite all to come unto Christ, 4) assist the bishop with temporal things, and 5) fellowship quorum members and other young men. Explain how you are doing on each of these duties, and set a goal to help you fulfill each of them. How can I enhance the self-esteem of girls and women that I come in contact with, and what would a compliment do for their self-image? What sort of words would Heavenly Father say to them if He were helping me know what to say? What does it mean to "Put on the Whole Armor of God?" – Ephesians 6.
- ✓ Fun - My favorite thing that happened at ManCamp was…
- ✓ Photo Page

NOTES:

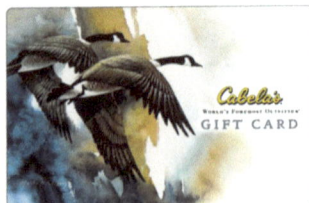

Selecting a Camp Spot

The ideal camp spot could be debated indefinitely, but for our purposes, we want to prioritize a spot based on several factors. Weather is the first factor to consider. If it were winter, a bluff to break the wind facing south would be ideal. Bugs are another factor. If you camp in low laying areas, you may be closer to standing water, which will mean, more bugs, especially at dusk. Performing a thorough check for ant hills is another very wise suggestion. Risking a goodnights sleep to a steam that never goes quiet might be another factor, so camping by a waterfall is unadvisable. Likewise, if it is fresh water, remember the wildlife that have probably been drinking there long before you arrived, so check for tracks, especially predator tracks. You would hate to discover the wolf pack drinking hole is your next door neighbor.

Are you in a watershed collection area? Does the water run through your campsite? You might want to relocate a few sea level feet higher, and choose another spot.

Write 2 Letters to your Son

Prior to camp you will need to write 2 letters to your son.

Letter 1 - Apologize for taking his extra can of beans, and for dumping his water out, as will be explained below.

Letter 2 - Congratulate him for surviving his challenge. Apologize for making him think it was going to be 3 days, telling him it was just for effect, and congratulate him for completing his survival challenge.

Take his Food and Water

This part might be one of the most painful of them all. On the midmorning of the first day, you gave your son 2 cans of beans to tide him over. When night comes, and he is sound asleep you must go to his supplies and take the second can away, the one he did not eat for supper. Next you must throw away any other left-overs he had from that night into the trash or the fire (or eat it yourself). You also need to dump his water out except for a few drops. You must leave him a note explaining that it was you that had to take it from him, but that it was to symbolize bugs getting into his food, or his food turning rancid. Remind him that last year he learned to live off of food found in the environment, and that this year, he must do that or starve.

Learning to Store Food

In nature, as in life, your fortune can turn in the blink of an eye. Teach your son to tie his pack and food on a tree limb as shown in the picture below. The branch should be solid and be at least 10 feet high, 10 feet from the trunk of the tree, and 4 feet from the branch the food is hanging from. When we are careless with our resources, they may be taken from us.

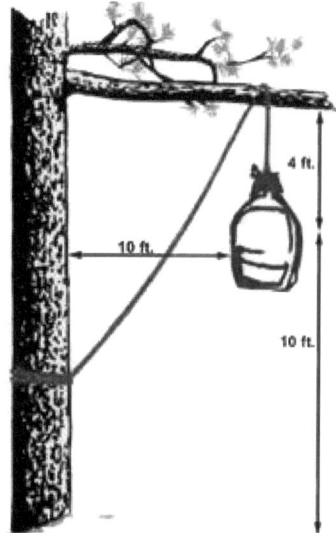

Obviously you will never jeopardize your son's health, but you must do this so he can really know what it feels like to be truly hungry. I believe this is one of the most life changing experiences you can provide for your son. Do not let him cut corners, and challenge him to use the knowledge he already has to find food. I remind you, this is the year he will learn the most about himself. How he responds will be a direct reflection of the man he will one day become. Tell him that today he can whine, cry, sit, work, swim, or whatever he wants. He can be mad at you, he can ask to quit, he may even snap, hunger can do this to a person. Remind him that he can do it. You believe in him, and that it is not to be cruel but for him to learn something about himself! He can emerge triumphant in the face of adversity, he can conquer.

It is highly advisable that you participate, let him know that you are not going to eat anything until his challenge is done, that way it will bond you rather than divide you. Seeing you suffer alongside him will let him know that you will stand by him in all things. If he asks when the challenge is over, remind him that it is a 3 day challenge, and the more he thinks about the easy meal, the less he will learn.

At night he will have settled into the notion that he is going to have to go to bed hungry. At about 5pm, hand him the second letter with a smile. I would advise putting his $100 Cabela's gift card in with this letter, but that is optional.

Get some supper, you earned it too!

Recap
Day 1

7:00	a.m.	Let him eat a good camp breakfast, encourage him to eat until he is stuffed.
7:30	a.m.	Remind him to eat up, it will be a long day. When he is completely done eating and cleaning up, hand him 2 cans of beans and a canteen of water, and tell him this is all he gets for the next 3 days, and you are going to do the same, as a survival challenge.
5:00	p.m.	Eat your beans with him.
10:00	p.m.	Take the rest of his beans, and dump out his water, leave the note as explained above.

Day 2

7:00	a.m.	He will awaken to no food or water.
7:30	a.m.	Forage for food, and get some water.
5:00	p.m.	Hand him the 2nd letter.
5:01	p.m.	Eat Up.

Spiritual Lessons
Poisoned by Degrees
This lesson can be fun by the campfire. Give your son a cup of hot chocolate, when your son takes his first small sip, tell him you saw a bat fly overhead while you were making the hot chocolate, and that you saw something fall right near his cup on the table. At first you were sure it was a bug or something, but now, upon reflecting upon it, it was probably some poo. As he tries to spit out the sip, laugh and tell him you were kidding.

Say, "you know, you could have probably drank that entire cup thinking it was delicious, and the poo could have completely dissolved; maybe not, it could have just stewed at the bottom." Give another laugh, and reassure him that you were just kidding-again.

Now is the time for teaching. You could say, "You know, the Book of Mormon talks about bat poo, well not exactly, but it does talk about being poisoned by degrees. Do you know what that is?" Let your son answer, and if he is on target let him talk,

62

if not, redirect him by proceeding.

Say, "Being poisoned by degrees is a way someone can become de-sensitized to a poison. It comes in small doses so the victim doesn't even know it, only to be discovered when the victim is dying. You have probably heard about how lobsters cook best by putting them in cold water and slowing raising the temperature until it is boiling. You have probably heard the lesson about, would you drink a Slurpee if it only had a little puke in it- haven't you? Of course the answer is no, but we often act as though the answer is yes." You see, Satan doesn't like to do a full frontal assault. He likes to poison us by degrees. How does he do that?" Let your son answer, and talk about his experiences, if any.

Continue by saying, "Satan likes to expose us to things. He will give us an amazing cake, and add just a little dog poo in the icing. What would that be? Consider a movie that is family friendly for 99%, just to throw in one cuss word. Who is offended by just one cuss word? So [G] rated movies are ok, then what happens. A little more dog poo, and add a little cat puke in the dough. Who will taste it when it is cooked-right? So we might see a movie that has 2 cuss words, and an inappropriate joke, after all, hell and damn are in the bible aren't they? You see, Satan will proceed in this fashion. He will desensitize you if you let him. Soon you find yourself justifying content in movies with phrases like, it is only one sex scene and it is only [PG-13], or it is only [R] because there is a lot of war fighting, there is no sex in it, as though the ½ puke is ok if mixed with ½ Slurpee. Satan will expose you, and make you more resistant to his poisons. Your tolerance for his poison will be great, and then when confronted with pornography, you will have built up a resistance so great that even that seems to not be too corrosive. What types of things can we do to recognize the spirit and stay clear of Satan's poison? Let your son answer, and talk about his experiences, if any.

Testify. You could say, "Satan is the father of all lies. He seeks to destroy you. In hunting terms, you are a 10 point buck. You are almost old enough to serve a mission. You are old enough to have a baby of your own; you are a man in almost every sense of the word. Satan would destroy your happiness by tempting you, by poisoning you by stopping you in any way he can. He does not want you to honor your priesthood, because he is jealous of you. He does not want you to be ready and worthy to serve a mission. He does not want you worthy to marry a young lady in the temple. He wants to destroy you, and will stop at nothing to do it. Do not allow him to poison you by degrees. Keep yourself worthy. If you make a mistake, the Savior Jesus Christ can save you. Just as you would not want to drink bat poo hot chocolate, or dog poo iced cake, or puke Slurpee, avoid the things that offend the spirit. Be watchful of the things you take into your spirit. Take only clean things into your mind. God has a great work for you in store. You are a great young man, and I love you, I am proud to be called your father. I testify that God is real, He is all powerful, and He wants you to be happy. Keep His commandments and you will find happiness in this life, and the life to come. You will be counted worthy at the last day to stand in his presence, I so testify in the name of Jesus Christ, Amen."

At this point, I usually give my son a hug. If your conversation goes as it should you will want to. Let that linger. I usually give it a few minutes before I return to my usual joking self.

Alma 47:18
"And it came to pass that Amalickiah caused that one of his servants should administer poison by degrees to Lehonti, that he died."

Satan works in the same way, he poisons us by degrees.

The Beggar
Where we camp it is not a national forest, so occasionally a peanut or two has been known to fall and quickly be picked up by a squirrel. Along come lakes you can sometimes throw a little fish food and let the fish guppy up and eat. Near certain eating establishments you will find seagulls, and throwing them a french fry

can be fun. You can introduce your short spiritual lesson in a number of ways but an animal begging for more has always been a good one for me.

After feeding a couple of nuts, say to your son, "We are all beggars like these little guys, you know. We beg just like this for blessings from Heavenly Father. We wait for Him to give blessings to us. We often do very little work, and expect Him to do everything for us. Imagine if these little guys could take the seeds we are giving them, and have the will power to plant them, rather than eat them up.

God works that way. If we take what he gives us, and we are able to multiply what he gives us, this is what He calls, 'bearing fruit.' If we bear good fruit, we are what he calls, 'profitable servants.' Think of it like this. If God gave you $1 and told you to do something with it, and you opened a lemonade stand and were able to take the $1 and turn it into $5, he would be really pleased. Imagine if he gave you $20, and you turned it into $1,000, he would be happy. Now if you were given $1 Million dollars and turned it into a Trillion, he would entrust you with everything that he has. That is how he lets us learn in this life. He gives us a little, and sees what we do with it. If we are wise stewards of what He has given us, he magnifies us, and gives us more. You can be a profitable steward. I have seen it already with how you share your testimony at church, pay your tithing, say your prayers, and serve others. You are on the right track, and even though you are just a boy, others will see your good works, and know you are boy who serves the Lord.

Look at our blessings. We can read and write we have knowledge of the gospel; we have a great place to live, a car, a TV. and so forth. Imagine if we took all that Heavenly Father gave us and gave it to His cause. Imagine if we decided to consecrate all our efforts, skills, money, and talents-everything, to building up His kingdom?"

You know a man approached Jesus and the man told Jesus he had kept all the commandments from his youth, and wondered what he could do more. Jesus looked at the man, and told him to sell all that he hath, give it to the poor, and come follow Him. Jesus issues us the same challenge. We can't take any of the possessions we have with us to heaven, but we can take all the knowledge we gain in this life with us. This is what is meant by, where your treasure is, there will your heart be also. What do we treasure in this life? Do we want praise from the world, credit for our good deeds? We should seek to always do the Lord's will especially when no one is looking. The Lord taught us, pray in secret that the Lord may bless thee in abundance. We shouldn't sound a trumpet when we give the bishop our tithing, we shouldn't seek recognition for our good deeds. The Lord told us, we have our reward. I don't know about you, but I would rather lay treasures up in heaven. The Lord told us, lay up your treasures in heaven where the thief cannot steal, and moth doth not corrupt. This means we can keep our blessings and treasures if they are done for God. We can lay treasures up in store. How do you think we can lay treasures up in store?"

Let your son give you some ideas and build on them for a minute or two.

End this with a short testimony. Something like, "I know God will bless us if we keep His commandments. He will bless us with riches in this life if we seek to do good with it. He will prosper you with riches, talents and blessings. You have been greatly blessed of the Lord, I hope and pray you will always use what He gives you, and you chose to plant it, you chose to magnify it, you chose to build His Kingdom. I know that as you do this, He will make a great man out of you, and he already has started. You are a good boy, and I love you!" I always try to pat my son on the back at this point. I let the silence work for a moment, then I say, "Looks like the fire needs another log, can you do that for me son?"

I wait a minute or so after the log is thrown on and say, "Have you thought about what kind of life you want to live? What sorts of things you want out of life, what goals you have?"

St. Mathew 25: 34-40
34 Then shall the King say unto them on his right hand, Come, ye blessed of my Father, inherit the kingdom prepared for you from the foundation of the world:
35 For I was an hungred, and ye gave me meat: I was thirsty, and ye gave me drink: I was a stranger, and ye took me in:
36 Naked, and ye clothed me: I was sick, and ye visited me: I was in prison, and ye came unto me.
37 Then shall the righteous answer him, saying, Lord, when saw we thee an hungred, and fed thee? or thirsty, and gave thee drink?
38 When saw we thee a stranger, and took thee in? or naked, and clothed thee?
39 Or when saw we thee sick, or in prison, and came unto thee?
40 And the King shall answer and say unto them, Verily I say unto you, Inasmuch as ye have done it unto one of the least of these my brethren, ye have done it unto me.

2 Nephi 1:20
20 And he hath said that: Inasmuch as ye shall keep my commandments ye shall prosper in the land; but inasmuch as ye will not keep my commandments ye shall be cut off from my presence.

Treasure your Blessings
This lesson goes well with the challenge assigned for age 13. As you son is thinking about his stomach, maybe angry, or grumpy, ask your son, "If you knew your food was going to get stolen, would you have done anything differently?" Let him answer, hopefully he says something like, 'I would have tied in higher, or I would have slept with it, or I would have eaten it all last night,' which are all great responses. Ask him if he would like to hear a story to take his mind off of things for a few minutes. Start by saying, "Since you see that your fortune can change in an instant, do you think this can be like life?" Let him answer, and hopefully his responses can help guide you. I try to build on his responses by saying, "this experience is a lot like life. Do you think the guy who gets in an accident and suddenly ends up in a wheel chair planned it that way? Or do you suppose the man who loses his wife to cancer, or his daughter to a swimming pool has any pre-planning? Life is going to throw you a lot of curve balls. Perhaps your lot will be different than mine, or others, but you will have them. Not everyone lives a charmed life. Some kids come from bad homes, some from abusive homes; do you think they planned that? Some might wonder if there is a God at all with all the terrible problems of our day. Some will view their lot in life, and feel like cursing God, and renouncing His very existence.

God is not vindictive. He does not allow us to suffer for nothing. Think of life like a giant checkers game. When you were 6 you thought you were pretty good. When you were 9, you were sure you were good. When you are 9 and you play an old grandpa what do you suppose happens?" Let him answer.

Proceed with, "the grandpa is no better at checkers than a 9 year old, he just sees more. The rules are still the same; he just has a greater vision of the end. That is how we get better; by learning from old men,

and that is how we learn in this life. Just like in checkers, we don't 'see' as much of the game as our grandfathers, but we must realize they know more than we do. God operates in much the same manner.

Pain, suffering, misfortune, are all learning opportunities. How much empathy can one man who lost his wife to cancer offer another man who is losing his wife to cancer? Jesus Christ suffered for all our sins; therefore he is the perfect judge. Jesus is a man who has literally walked <u>every</u> mile in <u>every</u> man's shoes.

You will never know what it is like to be the Savior, but you can perhaps empathize a little with the kids you see on those telethon promotions to raise money for starving children after today.

You can't always control the good and bad in your life, but you can control how you react to it. When you have it bad, I recommend you read in the bible about a man named Job. His story is amazing. He had it all, all was taken from him, and then in the end, he had it all restored to him."

Testify. "In your life, you will have a lot of good, and a lot of bad. Rejoice in the good, and accept the bad. Just as a young child submits his Father in all things, so too should we submit to the will of our Father in Heaven. God is watching over you, He will help you on your way. His lessons are like an old wise checkers player, and the quicker we can seek to learn His ways, the happier we will find ourselves in this life. I love the Lord, and I love you. May you receive God's choicest blessings all the days of your life, and may you learn to accept the lessons He desires you to have, in the name of Jesus Christ, Amen."

PREPARATION:

- ✓ Pray and study your scriptures and ask the Lord to bless you as you seek to connect your son to his gospel.
- ✓ Fast the Sunday before ManCamp asking for the Lord's blessing.
- ✓ Purchase a few sheets of malleable tin or copper from the hardware store (or my website).
- ✓ Research – Fasting and Blessings (Topical Guide)
- ✓ See Spiritual Lessons – Is there a God, or Am I talking to the Wind, and The Mountain Stream.
- ✓ Check the website www.raisingboysintomen.com to see if there are any videos you may need to watch to prepare.
- ✓ Invite mommy to say a prayer right before you leave for ManCamp, asking Heavenly Father to keep her boys in safety.

CHALLENGE:

- ✓ 2 day survival with 1 can of beans, sleeping bag, Survival Knife
- ✓ Learn to safely use an axe.
- ✓ Read 50 pages of scripture.
- ✓ Record his testimony on sheets of tin or copper.
- ✓ Invite him to set a goal to become an Elder and marry to the right person in the right place at the right time.

REWARD:

- ✓ A 12-gauge shotgun. Get a good one, he will have it FOREVER!

JOURNAL:

- ✓ Mental – Am I reading from the best books, aside from my studies at school, if so, what? What do I want to read this year?
- ✓ Physical – Wearing clean appropriate clothes is a reflection of how I feel about myself, and is a reflection of my feelings about God. How have I been doing? Do I have any areas to improve upon? This year at home, start doing your own laundry if you have not already done so.
- ✓ Spiritual – the duties of a teacher are to 1) set a proper example, 2) be a good home teacher, 3) greet the members at the church, 4) prepare the sacrament, 5) help at home, and 6) be a peacemaker Explain how you are doing on each of these duties, and set a goal to help you fulfill each of them. How can I enhance the self-esteem of girls and women that I come in contact with? What would a compliment do for their self-image? What sort of words would Heavenly Father say to them if He were helping me know what to say?
- ✓ Fun - My favorite thing that happened at ManCamp was…
- ✓ Photo Page

NOTES:

2-Day Survival

Now is a great opportunity for your son to showcase to himself that he has mastered all the requisite skills to survive on his own. This year he needs to complete two days of living off the land. He may have 1 can of beans, but the rest of his edibles should be found in nature.

Retain his Ability to Think Clearly under Pressure

Remind him to retain his faculties about him and to think of the best order to complete his tasks. For instance, you might remind him that he should as quickly as possible locate a fresh water drinking source. He will hopefully know enough to locate water, build a shelter, gather wood, and gather as much food as possible from nature. During this camp, it might be a good time to introduce him to a great pine needle broth. Gather about 5 handfuls of fresh green pine needles; put them in a pot of boiling water. Let it steep, and sip on your hot vitamin C rich broth for your evening treat. If your son has learned his lesson, he has secured his can of beans, or eaten them by the first night (remember, you took them last year). This year is a great year, he is officially a boy becoming a man.

Using an Axe

If you have the means, you should purchase a set of steel toed boots for your son for this camp. Having a solid boot on your foot enables you to complete a myriad of tasks with limited risk. Though it is a risky activity, your son is old enough to successfully wield an axe. At first teach him to hold the axe and swing with a wide foot stance. Always chop wood on a slight incline. Decline chopping = leg chopping, and is a big no-no.

Scripture Read

Let him wander off on his own. He will read some of the time, and some of the time he will probably throw pebbles at the tree. No matter how he uses his time, some of it will be reading the scriptures, and there is no better place to feel the quiet whisperings of the spirit than in the quiet forest surrounded by the beauty of God's creations. Invite him to record his testimony and life goals on the small 5x7 sheets of tin you brought. Have these framed, and display them somewhere in your home later.

Is God there or am I talking to the Wind?
While on the hike when you reach the top of a big hill or a mountain, I like to take the opportunity to yell something, "Hamilton Boy's Rule," or "Hamilton Men Can Conquer Anything," are pretty common phrases. Occasionally a loud Tarzan level crescendo can be heard (sorry if I scared away the bird you were looking at, if you happened to be hiking near me last time). Encourage your son to let his voice go, to yell as loud as he wants. After my fill of yelling, I like to sit on a rock and crack out some trail mix, and some water. Now is the time for teaching. After a few minutes of small talk, I say, "listen to the breeze. Awesome isn't it? Breathe that air. Heavenly Father made a nice place for us to climb. Let's see if we scared away all the wildlife, do you hear any?" Let him answer.

Then I say, "you know, Heavenly Father can yell at us like we just yelled. He doesn't do it often, he likes to give us small whispers. Do you know what that is like?" Let your son answer, and talk about his experiences, if any.

Then say, "rather than yelling Heavenly Father likes to whisper to us. You have probably heard the word, prompting-haven't you?" Let your son answer, and talk about his promptings, if he has had any in the past.

Say, "Heavenly Father likes to give us promptings. Often times they come to us as some random thought or something we should do or say. Promptings come, and as we learn to feel and recognize them, we are invited to obey. When we obey a prompting, we are serving Heavenly Father. When we serve Him, He is able to magnify our efforts, and more promptings come. The Lord loves a willing servant! When we receive a prompting, we should act immediately on it. Often times if we don't we start to think about it, and can be discouraged. If we feel we should invite someone to church, we should quickly do so. If we delay acting on the prompting, doubts and fears can creep in, those are not from Heavenly Father. His will is never filled with doubt, only courage. Have you ever delayed a prompting, only to miss out on the opportunity? Let your son answer, and talk about his experiences, if any, discuss them.

Then say, "There comes a time in everyone's life when they know they have received promptings, and they have said prayers, and they have had good feelings, but they can't say of a surety that God has spoken to them. Sometimes we may wonder, are we speaking to the wind? Is there really a God? If so, does He know me? These are all natural feelings. We have learned of the promptings the Spirit can offer, and we must ask, and learn for ourselves that there is a God. We must listen to our minds, our hearts, and our guts to know that there is a God. I know two things for sure about God, He exists and He loves me. My answer came when I sought Him in diligent prayer. For some it may come as a feeling inside that is indescribable, for some it may be a sign, for some a voice, for some a thought. The spirit will confirm it to you, and you can know for yourself. Have you ever felt sometimes like, is there a God? Let your son answer, and talk about his experiences, if any.

Say, "Sometimes people misinterpret God. I have sometimes prayed for things, and sometimes I feel like God ignores me. Maybe, what I am praying for isn't his will, but it is more likely a situation where God trust my ability to make decisions. As we align our lives with God's will, He will trust us to make decisions. This is why the Lord has taught us to council WITH Him not TO Him. As we put our lives in line with His will and obey His commandments, we are able to act for ourselves. When you are a boy, you ask if it is ok to go potty? When you are older, you ask, is it ok to go to a friend's house, and when you are yet older, you might ask, can I have $20 and the keys. These are all questions your Earthly Father can answer, and are appropriate for the stage that you are at. Heavenly Father wants us to council WITH Him. We need to grow, and part of that growth is learning to make decisions in harmony with His will and seeking His will in all things. Think about it, did Jesus have to ask His Father if it was ok to heal the blind man? Of course not! He knew the will of His Father, and it is up to us to learn how to live our lives so that we can always perform our duties in this life in harmony with His will, just as Jesus did. How do you think God will answer you? Have you already had that experience? Let your son answer, and talk about his experiences, if any.

Testify. Say something like, "God hears and answers prayers. He wants to have a personal relationship with you. As you seek Him, and as you seek to do His will in this life, you find great happiness. You will come to know, as I know, that He is a loving Father in Heaven and He wants to bless you! God is real, I so testify in the name of Jesus Christ. Amen.

I like to let the spirit linger for a moment of two, then, at this point I usually give a push to my son, or throw a pebble at him. You can do anything that can break up the conversation in a fun loving way.

John 3:16
For God so loved the world, that he gave his only begotten Son, that whosoever believeth in him should not perish, but have everlasting life.

Alma 37:12
"... for he doth counsel in wisdom over all his works, and his paths are straight, and his course is one eternal round."

PREPARATION:
- ✓ Pray and study your scriptures and ask the Lord to bless you as you seek to connect your son to his gospel.
- ✓ Fast the Sunday before ManCamp asking for the Lord's blessing.
- ✓ Research
- ✓ See Spiritual Lessons –All are Equal unto God, Is there a God, or am I Talking to the Wind (see age 14), and A Mountain Stream (see ages 3-5)
- ✓ Check the website www.raisingboysintomen.com to see if there are any videos you may need to watch to prepare.
- ✓ Invite mommy to say a prayer right before you leave for ManCamp, asking Heavenly Father to keep her boys in safety.

CHALLENGE:
- ✓ 5 mile pack in camp.
- ✓ Read 100 pages of scripture.
- ✓ Invite your son to seek his Patriarchal Blessing.
- ✓ Reaffirm a goal to serve a mission and to marry in the temple.

REWARD:
- ✓ $100 in cash to do with as he chooses.

JOURNAL:
- ✓ Mental – Have I given strong consideration about what I would like to do for a living when I am a grown man? Where are my interests, where would I be successful? How will I support a family? Research a career you might do when you are grown, and write a report.
- ✓ Physical – Am I exercising regularly? What goals do I have for my physical body for this year? **Hint, Hint, you can date next year; you might want to hunk up a little…I am just saying.
- ✓ Spiritual – Memorize the sacrament prayer for the bread. How can I avoid pornography in all its forms and support the chastity of women? How can I show the Lord I am willing to obey his commandments when I am surrounded by so many pressures?
- ✓ Fun - My favorite thing that happened at ManCamp was…
- ✓ Photo Page

NOTES:

Atonement

The objective of this camp is to ensure your son knows what the atonement of Jesus Christ is, and how to use it. Teach him how to ask the Lord for true forgiveness, and what the Savior of the world did for him in in the Garden of Gethsemane and on the Cross. Teach him to love and emulate the life and teachings of the Lord Jesus Christ. Testify of the Plan of Salvation and that God has a purpose for us.

He is an accomplished camper at this point, there is no disputing that. This year he will learn what is really important, and what can be done without. Teenagers these days have abundance, and this year he will be quickly reminded what a necessity is, and what a luxury is. This camp is just a fun time, enjoy yourself! Have a few sling shot shoot offs, and take the time to talk to your son. Spending time with him will give you the opportunity to ask him how things are going. Ask him about school, about church, about his friends, and about where he is headed in life. Now is the perfect time to listen. Listening is the key. He will have a lot of things on his mind, let him unload. Be very slow to offer council and judgment this year. At 15 he is not ready for a sermon or to be lectured, he is ready to be heard, so bite your tongue; he will figure most of his own problems out. Ask questions, be engaged and interested in his worries. Not many years ago, you were in his same shoes! Be patient, encouraging, and listen, that will mean more than any lessons you could teach him.

Hike

On day 2, go on a short hike to a spring or a stream, or a small mountain. When you are at the top, remind him of the beauty of nature. Remind him that you are glad that Heavenly Father created such wonders. This is a great opportunity to offer a brief testimony. Remind him of some of the things he shared, let him know that you have been thinking about what he said. Reassure him that you know that God will help him as he is keeping the commandments. As you share a SHORT testimony, ask him if he believes God has the power to see him through his troubles? Reassure him that God has that power. Remind him of the power of the Savior. Jesus can and will forgive him, and that the atonement is real. 15 is not the 15 of old. He has probably seen some pornography, and he has probably dabbled in sin. He has probably been taken for a bit of a ride by Satan. It is important that this year, you are a listening and reassuring party. Testify to him that if he ever loses his way in this life that the Savior Jesus Christ knew he would sin and fall short of perfection, and that he prepared a way to return through the atonement. Let him know how proud you are of him, and let him know you have confidence he will find his way, if he stays close to the Lord, reads his scriptures, says he prayers, and repents on his knees when he has done wrong.

Now is a great time, if you have not already done so, to encourage your son to receive his Patriarchal blessing. You may need to explain lineage, and this is a great year to teach the Spiritual thought about Abraham and Sand, if you have not already taught it.

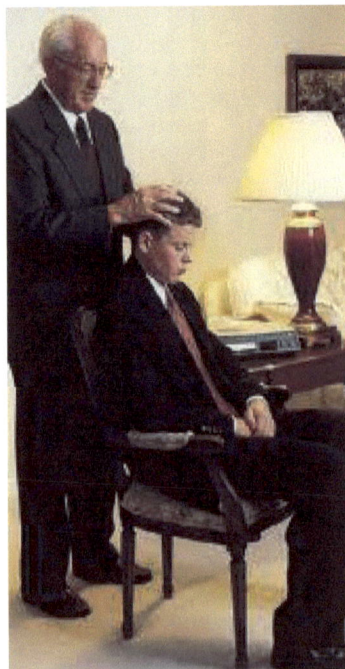

Spiritual Lessons
All Are Equal unto God
While you are walking and see some wild flowers side by side, ask your son, "Which of these two flowers do you think Heavenly Father likes the most?" Let him answer, and explain his reasoning. Ask, "Do you think God loves some people more than others?"

If your son thinks God does, then ask him a question that might baffle him. If he says he thinks God loves roses more than Daisy's because God's favorite color is Red, than ask him, "why didn't God just make all Daisy's red then?" This can be a fun game, but be careful, if you son has a quick wit, you might find yourself convinced of God's preferences.

If your son believes God loves all his creations equally you might say, "ah, so you see that God loves variety? Why do you think that is?" Let your son answer, and talk about his reasons if possible.
Continue with, "So if God loves a rose as much as he loves a daisy, do you think he loves a bad man as much as he loves a good man?" Let your son answer, and talk if he is willing.

As you discuss bad men and good, ask him if people generally treat others as God would treat them. Hopefully he has noticed at this point that people often do not treat each other with a great deal of equality.

Say, "so if God loves everyone, why do we sometimes judge others? If someone hasn't taken a bath in a while, do we sometimes think that the person is a grub, and worthy of less respect? How about a homeless person, or a person in jail?"

You know Jesus talked about this, he taught us the two great commandments. They are, "love God with all your heart, and love your neighbor as yourself." If we begin to see people with their full potential as sons and daughters of God, no less worthy of the crown you and I can inherit, we can begin to help them live up to their divine inheritance.

Judging others can be dangerous, because Jesus taught that how we judge others will be how we are judged. We should only judge righteously.

The Lord has a tendency to select rough stones and malleable young servants. Paul the apostle was one of the worst persecutors of the church, so was Alma the younger. The Lord selected the boy prophet Samuel, the boy prophet Mormon; the boy prophet David; the boy prophet Nephi; the boy prophet Joseph of Egypt; and the boy prophet Joseph Smith, all of which were your age. The Lord has a knack of polishing and pressing coal to create His diamonds. That is why when we see a rough stone we should not dismiss it as a thing of no worth because the Lord through his furnace of affliction can cleanse purify and qualify any man for his work. As you let the Lord polish you, you will be capable of a great many things.

Testify. You could say, "Every man on this earth is capable of becoming a smooth polished stone with God's help. Every man has rough edges that need to be polished, and beneath everyman's coal is a diamond waiting to be shined. God loves all men equally, and God could sure use you."

Is there a God, or am I Talking to the Wind
(see age 14)

A Mountain Stream
(see ages 3-5)

St. John 4: 13-14
13 Jesus answered and said unto her, Whosoever drinketh of this water shall thirst again:

14 But whosoever drinketh of the water that I shall give him shall never thirst; but the water that I shall give him shall be in him a well of water springing up into everlasting life.

Doctrine and Covenants 20: 77-79
Bread

> *"O God, the Eternal Father, we ask thee in the name of thy Son, Jesus Christ, to bless and sanctify this bread to the souls of all those who partake of it, that they may eat in remembrance of the body of thy Son, and witness unto thee, O God, the Eternal Father, that they are willing to take upon them the name of thy Son, and always remember him and keep his commandments which he has given them; that they may always have his Spirit to be with them. Amen."*

Water

> *"O God, the Eternal Father, we ask thee in the name of thy Son, Jesus Christ, to bless and sanctify this [water] to the souls of all those who drink of it, that they may do it in remembrance of the blood of thy Son, which was shed for them; that they may witness unto thee, O God, the Eternal Father, that they do always remember him, that they may have his Spirit to be with them. Amen."*

PREPARATION:

- ✓ Pray and study your scriptures and ask the Lord to bless you as you seek to connect your son to his gospel.
- ✓ Fast the Sunday before ManCamp asking for the Lord's blessing.
- ✓ Research The Oath and Covenant of the Priesthood.
- ✓ See Spiritual Lessons – The Oath and Covenant of the Priesthood.
- ✓ Check the website www.raisingboysintomen.com to see if there are any videos you may need to watch to prepare.
- ✓ Invite mommy to say a prayer right before you leave for ManCamp, asking Heavenly Father to keep her boys in safety.

CHALLENGE:

- ✓ Finish any Eagle Scout Projects as needed
- ✓ Read the Book of Mormon for 8 hours
- ✓ Invite him to pray about what he has read, and to ask God if they are true as instructed in Moroni 10:3-5.
- ✓ Invite him to share the gospel with someone, and to reaffirm his goals to serve a mission, and to marry in the temple.

REWARD:

- ✓ A rifle of his choosing .30-06, .223, .270 are great choices

JOURNAL:

- ✓ Mental – Have I given strong consideration about what I would like to do for a living when I am a grown man? Where are my interests, where would I be successful? How will I support a family? Research a career you might do when you are grown, and write a report.
- ✓ Physical – Am I exercising regularly? What goals do I have for my physical body for this year?
- ✓ Spiritual – the duties of a priest are to 1) teach the gospel, 2) baptize, 3) administer the sacrament, 4) visit the members, 5) ordain others to the Aaronic Priesthood, and 6) assist in missionary work. What do these duties mean? Memorize the sacrament prayer for the water. How can I feel and recognize the spirit to be prepared for missionary service?
- ✓ Testimony
- ✓ Fun - My favorite thing that happened at ManCamp was…
- ✓ Photo Page

NOTES:

Write a Letter

Prior to camp you should write your son a letter to be delivered at camp. In the letter commend him for the good things he has been doing, address any small areas of concern briefly, but do not emphasize them. Tell him how you have been impressed with his recent accomplishments, and that you are very proud of him. If he is close to his Eagle Scout award, plan this camp to meet and complete any final tasks he has left. This is a big year for him! Help him tie off any loose ends he may have, and use this year as an opportunity to spend some time with him. He has a 10 hour challenge to read his scriptures, encourage him to read from the Book of Mormon, but any scriptures will do. The point is for him to immerse himself in nature, and learn to really feel the spirit.

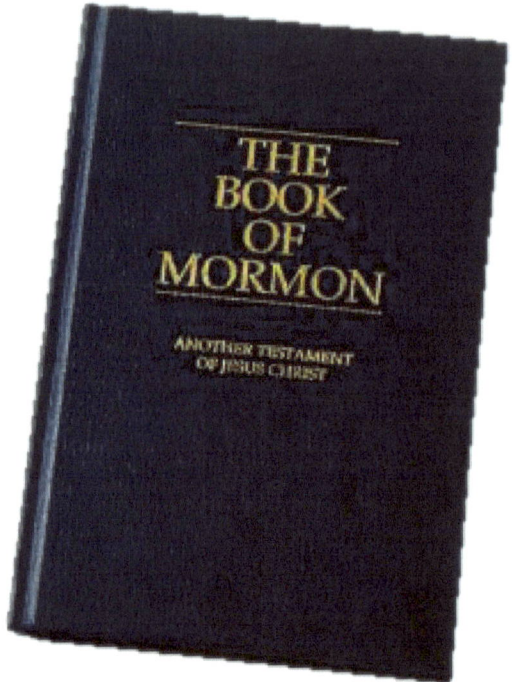

Ask

At supper you might ask him what he is reading about, and ask him to tell the story. Ask him what lessons are to be learned from what he read. Ask him how he feels? Attempt to help him recognize the spirit, but do not push the issue, he will feel the spirit in his own time, in his own way.

Encourage him to take a short solo hike, let him know you will take care of his dishes. Seek any opportunity to serve him, as this year, he will commune with God in nature, by himself, you best not get in the way! Ask him if he has thought of serving his Father in Heaven by going on a mission. Do not pressure, just ask, and let him work it out. Pressure is the LAST thing you want to EVER do!

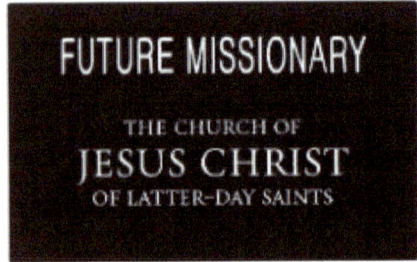

Testify of the blessings that await him, should he decide to serve.

Spiritual Lessons
The Oath and Covenant of the Priesthood
This can be a good night conversation, often around the campfire, and this lesson is often reserved for a boy 16-18ish.

You could inquire, "Have you given any thought to what you want to do for a living when you are out on your own?" Let him answer, and build on his responses. Ask him questions, and listen. He may not have given it much thought to this point, but he might have a few ideas that interest him.

Ask, "Have you given any thought to having a family of your own, what kind of girl you would like to marry?" Let him answer, but this might be a little touchy if he is dating or not dating, so make it a point to listen, ask, but don't pry.

You could continue, "Have you given more thought about serving the Lord on a mission?" Let him answer, and if he has already set the goal, great, but if he has not, you should not give a lecture about expectations. Missionary service needs to be a decision he makes, it has to be one he commits to. You should let the silence be your friend here; most people will talk if there is a prolonged silence. Give it a minute, he might open up. If he is ready, he will talk, if he is not, he will not, either way, it has him thinking.

One of the worst things you can do is pressure him at this point. Don't stare him down, relax and chill, look at the campfire. If the conversation goes well, and he is committed and excited to go on a mission, yippee, you have done a great job (either you or your wife) preparing him, save the last part of this lesson for later. If he has not committed, you might want to continue with this section.

You can begin by saying, "If I told you I was going to give you $500 in cash tomorrow, it might be a good idea to get it in writing, but would you need me to put it in writing?" Let your son answer and negotiate this in his mind, and you can have a brief discussion. After a minute or two, you could ask, "if I told you I was going to add you to my checking account, and sign the title of my vehicles over to you, could you be trusted with that kind of responsibility?" Again, let him answer. As you discuss the responsibilities involved, you might want to guide it to the next question.

Say, "Just as I believe I could entrust you with $100, my car, all my Earthly money, and even with my very life, those things are very minor compared to what you are almost of age to receive. What do you think the Melchizedec priesthood is?" Let him answer and answer any of his questions.

You might explain, "An oath is a sworn affirmation to be true and faithful to your promises. A covenant is a solemn promise between two parties. The Melchizedek Priesthood is received by an unspoken oath as well as by covenant. Those Priesthood holders who are faithful to the end and do all he asks of them will receive all that the Father has."

"As faithful followers of Jesus Christ, we must do all that is asked of us. We should seek to magnify our callings, testify to the world or the truth, and do all that is asked of us, in building His kingdom. When we receive the Oath and Covenant of the Priesthood, we should not take it lightly. Should we reject this oath, once it is taken, we will not receive forgiveness of sins in this life, or in the next."

"The Melchizedec Priesthood is a great blessing and a great responsibility. One day you will preside in your home. As the priesthood holder in your home you will need to set a spiritual example, and will be held accountable for the teaching of your children, and the council given to your wife. Just as God gives us responsibilities, he also makes you promises; you will always have sufficient for your needs."

Testify. You might say, "As your Father, I have done my best to teach you what you need to know. I hope and pray you serve the Lord in this life. By accepting the Melchizedek Priesthood, you take the Lords authority into the world with you, but you also take responsibly with it as well. The Lord will be with you. He will go before your face, and will be on your left hand and on your right; you will find happiness in staying close to the Lord, and in performing your duties while in his service. I hope and pray you find success as a missionary one day, and I know you will find great happiness in your life, should you decide to serve diligently. You are a fine son, I am proud of you, I love you, your mother loves you, and the Lord loves you, in the name of Jesus Christ, Amen."

You may want to give your son a hug.

Doctrine and Covenants 42:14
"And the Spirit shall be given unto you by the prayer of faith; and if ye receive not the Spirit ye shall not teach."

2 Nephi 32:3
Angels speak by the power of the Holy Ghost; wherefore, they speak the words of Christ. Wherefore, I said unto you, feast upon the words of Christ; for behold, the words of Christ will tell you all things what ye should do.

Moroni 10: 4-5
4 And when ye shall receive these things, I would exhort you that ye would ask God, the Eternal Father, in the name of Christ, if these things are not true; and if ye shall ask with a sincere heart, with real intent, having faith in Christ, he will manifest the truth of it unto you, by the power of the Holy Ghost.
5 And by the power of the Holy Ghost ye may know the truth of all things.

Mosiah 3:19
19 For the natural man is an enemy to God, and has been from the fall of Adam, and will be, forever and ever, unless he yields to the enticings of the Holy Spirit, and putteth off the natural man and becometh a saint through the atonement of Christ the Lord, and becometh as a child, submissive, meek, humble, patient, full of love, willing to submit to all things which the Lord seeth fit to inflict upon him, even as a child doth submit to his father.

1 Nephi 1:20
... behold, I, Nephi, will show unto you that the tender mercies of the Lord are over all those whom he hath chosen, because of their faith, to make them mighty even unto the power of deliverance.

Alma 43:2
2 Now we shall say no more concerning their preaching, except that they preached the word, and the truth, according to the spirit of prophecy and revelation; and they preached after the holy order of God by which they were called.

PREPARATION:
- ✓ Pray and study your scriptures and ask the Lord to bless you as you seek to connect your son to his gospel.
- ✓ Fast the Sunday before ManCamp asking for the Lord's blessing.
- ✓ Research – The meaning of becoming a Patriarch on LDS.org
- ✓ See Spiritual Lessons – Patriarch of your Home
- ✓ Check the website www.raisingboysintomen.com to see if there are any videos you may need to watch to prepare.
- ✓ Invite mommy to say a prayer right before you leave for ManCamp, asking Heavenly Father to keep her boys in safety.

CHALLENGE:
- ✓ Learn the basics of what a mission will entail.
- ✓ Give him a copy of Preach my Gospel, and go over the basics.
- ✓ Go on some hikes, take some swims, and enjoy the outdoors.
- ✓ Invite him to always live the commandments
- ✓ Read scriptures for 4 hours and Invite him to pray about what he has read, and to ask God if they are true as instructed in Moroni 10:3-5.
- ✓ Invite him to preside in his future family in love and righteousness as Patriarch of his future home.

REWARD:
- ✓ A handshake, and a good look in the eye, and a verbal, "congratulations on becoming a man." Give your boy a hug!

JOURNAL:
- ✓ Mental – Write a report on the career you are thing of pursuing someday.
- ✓ Physical – How is my diet, relaxation and exercise? Am I taking care of my temple?
- ✓ Spiritual – Read the Oath and Covenant of the Priesthood. The duties of the Melchizedec Priesthood are 1) be converted to the gospel of Jesus Christ, 2) teach your family, 3) family history and temple work, 4) welfare services, 5) missionary work, 6) home teaching, 7) quorum and church participation, and 8) community participation and service. How can I do to fulfill each area of responsibility? How does the spirit talk to me? Am I always in tune? If not, how can I improve? What does it mean to be the patriarch of my home?
- ✓ Fun - My favorite thing that happened at ManCamp was…
- ✓ Photo Page

NOTES:

Prior to camp you should write your son a letter to be delivered at camp. In the letter commend him for the fine son he has become. Let him know that you are pleased with him, and you hope he chooses to serve the Lord as a full-time missionary. It will be his choice, but tell him that greater blessings than he can now comprehend await him as he worthily and faithfully serve the Lord.

Spiritual Lessons
Patriarch of your Home
This lesson is reserved for the last ManCamp when your son is 17.
You might ask this by the campfire, or if the topic of your son's future career arises, you might decide to raise this topic. You could ask your son, "we have a lot of titles in our church don't you think? I mean we have hundreds. We have Bishops, Ward Mission Leader, Sunday School Teacher, Elder, Priest, Deacon, High Council, Stake President. Out of all the titles that we have in the church, which one do you think is the most important? Which one is probably the most important?" Your son might come up with some pretty great ideas here, but don't let his quick wit convince you, no matter how compelling his arguments, let him explain his reasoning though. He probably misinterpreted your question to mean, "jobs" in the church, not, "titles." Hey, if Captain Moroni can use stratagem to win, so can you-haha! When he is done, hopefully he asks you the same, but if not you can continue with this transition.

Say, "Of all the titles in the Church that is the most important, I would have to say, Father. Even Jesus deferred and reverenced above all else the name of his father. In his prayer he even said, 'Our Father, which art in Heaven, Hallowed be Thy name…" I know of no other way to earn a hallowed name. As patriarch in your home, one day you will have to preside. Have you given any thought to how you will teach your children right from wrong?" Let him answer and contemplate what you have said. Discuss his response.

You can continue if appropriate, "You know being a Father is a big responsibility. When you have kids, they are like sponges when they are little. It has sort of been a trend of society to balk at the responsibility, but the Lord must be greatly grieved. Marriage can be tough, even if you marry a near perfect person. There will be times when you might feel all is lost, and your marriage may hang in the balance. The casualties of divorce are always the children. That is what is meant by, 'the sins of the parents will be upon the children.' It is often a very conscious choice. You will have to decide what is most important. If you and your companion on a mission have a fight, transfers come soon, and you can say, adios. In marriage, especially eternal marriage, that is not the Lords way. The only cause of divorce is SELFISHNESS."

"I know society might try to tell you it is adultery or money problems, but those are still selfish. When you go to work, there will be dozens of times women in the office make themselves available to you. Some women are done up like it is prom, and you will go home to a wife who is wearing sweats who maybe hasn't showered, and has barf on her sleeve from your 4-year old. If your heart is not locked, you may find temptation creep in. You will need to have a deep love on those days. As you and your wife are acknowledging each other's positive efforts, you can survive anything."

"It is important to marry someone that is a hard worker. The worst person to possibly marry is a lazy person. No incentive can motivate them, avoid a lazy person like the plague."

"So your wife has puke on her sleeve, which can happen, but what about money? Didn't we say that was a reason? Well if you are having money problems, it is because you and your wife are not on the same team. If you or she buy things you can't afford, because you want them, you, or she are acting selfishly."

"Being a good husband and Father are a huge responsibility. The Savior taught us to be compassionate and loving, and above all, to be SELFLESS. Being a Father means, using your personal vacation days at work to take your son camping. Being a Father means, after a long day at work, you change your son's bike flat tire. Being a Father means, kneeling and getting your heart in the right place to give your son a blessing when he is sick. Being a Father means, setting the example by praying morning and night for your family. Being a good Husband means, supporting and sustaining your wife in all that she does in righteousness. Being a good Husband means, cleaning the toilet once in a while. Being a good Husband means, honoring your wife by locking your heart when other women attempt to steal it."

Testify. You might say, "Being the Patriarch in your own home someday is a big responsibility. If you stay close to the Lord, He will stay close to you. One day, you will have the title "Father" and I will get promoted to "Grand" and I know you will do a good job. I am very proud of you, you are a fine man! I know that God loves you, and wants the best for you as I do, in the sacred name of Jesus Christ, Amen."

This is the time that you congratulate your son with a hug. I recommend telling him, "you are officially a man, and a graduate of ManCamp. I am very proud of you. Come to me for council anytime, but now is your time to decide on what kind of life you want. I have taught you what I know, now it is time for you to decide what kind of man you want to be."

The Sandy Beach or Sandy area
Call your son over and tell him you would like to tell him a short story, but you can't tell the story until helps you do some counting. Clean off a large flat rock and lay it flat on the ground. Take a handful of sand from the shore and put it on one side of the flat rocks surface. Make a little pile of sand next to a larger pile of sand, and let him know you need him to count the grains of sand. Let him know you will be able to tell the story once you know how many grains of sand there are in the pile. As you count, have fun. Lose count once in a while and have fun and laugh with your son when he loses count or counts wrong. After about five minutes, ask him, "do you want to just quit and estimate this pile at 5,000?" He may want to keep counting, and if after 10-minutes of so you are still counting, you may need to fake a sneeze and mess up the piles. Laugh and say you are sorry, and that you will tell him the story since you messed up the piles. The story is as follows:

There are a lot of grains of sand on a beach, there are so many they could not be counted in a million lifetimes. Once there was a man that lived so righteously that he was promised by God that his posterity (children, grand-children, great grand-children, and great great grand-children, and great great great grand-children, and so on) would be so numerous that they would be greater than the sands of the sea. The man's name was Abraham, and the Lord promised Abraham that his children, and grand-children, and great grandchildren would number as the sands of the sea. Abraham was a righteous man, and he obeyed all of God's commandments. Sounds like a pretty awesome promise from God don't you think? (Let your son answer here). Well, let me tell you the cool part of the story. Abraham was in fact your Great Great Great Great ...(I let my voice trail off into a higher pitch after about 15 of these) Grand-Father and you are entitled to the same promises that God made to him. As a descendant of Abraham, this promise is also available to you. You can live your life righteously, and you can make covenants with Heavenly Father. Heavenly Father will make you the same promise, if you will obey his commandments. Pretty awesome, huh? Heavenly Father is really awesome! Now you know the story of your Great, Great, Great (repeat voice incline as above)...Grand-Father. God is super Awesome to make us such promises, don't you think?

At this point I usually start skipping rocks, or throwing rocks into the water, and let my son talk.

Doctrine and Covenants Section 84:40-111, 117-120.
(The Oath and Covenant of the Priesthood)
40 Therefore, all those who receive the priesthood, receive this oath and covenant of my Father, which he cannot break, neither can it be moved.
41 But whoso breaketh this covenant after he hath received it, and altogether turneth therefrom, shall not have forgiveness of sins in this world nor in the world to come.

42 And wo unto all those who come not unto this priesthood which ye have received, which I now confirm upon you who are present this day, by mine own voice out of the heavens; and even I have given the heavenly hosts and mine angels charge concerning you.

43 And I now give unto you a commandment to beware concerning yourselves, to give diligent heed to the words of eternal life.

44 For you shall live by every word that proceedeth forth from the mouth of God.

45 For the word of the Lord is truth, and whatsoever is truth is light, and whatsoever is light is Spirit, even the Spirit of Jesus Christ.

46 And the Spirit giveth light to every man that cometh into the world; and the Spirit enlighteneth every man through the world, that hearkeneth to the voice of the Spirit.

47 And every one that hearkeneth to the voice of the Spirit cometh unto God, even the Father.

48 And the Father teacheth him of the covenant which he has renewed and confirmed upon you, which is confirmed upon you for your sakes, and not for your sakes only, but for the sake of the whole world.

49 And the whole world lieth in sin, and groaneth under darkness and under the bondage of sin.

50 And by this you may know they are under the bondage of sin, because they come not unto me.

51 For whoso cometh not unto me is under the bondage of sin.

52 And whoso receiveth not my voice is not acquainted with my voice, and is not of me.

53 And by this you may know the righteous from the wicked, and that the whole world groaneth under sin and darkness even now.

54 And your minds in times past have been darkened because of unbelief, and because you have treated lightly the things you have received—

55 Which vanity and unbelief have brought the whole church under condemnation.

56 And this condemnation resteth upon the children of Zion, even all.

57 And they shall remain under this condemnation until they repent and remember the new covenant, even the Book of Mormon and the former commandments which I have given them, not only to say, but to do according to that which I have written—

58 That they may bring forth fruit meet for their Father's kingdom; otherwise there remaineth a scourge and judgment to be poured out upon the children of Zion.

59 For shall the children of the kingdom pollute my holy land? Verily, I say unto you, Nay.

60 Verily, verily, I say unto you who now hear my words, which are my voice, blessed are ye inasmuch as you receive these things;

61 For I will forgive you of your sins with this commandment—that you remain steadfast in your minds in solemnity and the spirit of prayer, in bearing testimony to all the world of those things which are communicated unto you.

62 Therefore, go ye into all the world; and unto whatsoever place ye cannot go ye shall send, that the testimony may go from you into all the world unto every creature.

63 And as I said unto mine apostles, even so I say unto you, for you are mine apostles, even God's high priests; ye are they whom my Father hath given me; ye are my friends;

64 Therefore, as I said unto mine apostles I say unto you again, that every soul who believeth on your words, and is baptized by water for the remission of sins, shall receive the Holy Ghost.

65 And these signs shall follow them that believe—

66 In my name they shall do many wonderful works;

67 In my name they shall cast out devils;

68 In my name they shall heal the sick;

69 In my name they shall open the eyes of the blind, and unstop the ears of the deaf;

70 And the tongue of the dumb shall speak;

71 And if any man shall administer poison unto them it shall not hurt them;

72 And the poison of a serpent shall not have power to harm them.

73 But a commandment I give unto them, that they shall not boast themselves of these things, neither speak them before the world; for these things are given unto you for your profit and for salvation.

74 Verily, verily, I say unto you, they who believe not on your words, and are not baptized in water in my name, for the remission of their sins, that they may receive the Holy Ghost, shall be damned, and shall not come into my Father's kingdom where my Father and I am.

75 And this revelation unto you, and commandment, is in force from this very hour upon all the world, and the gospel is unto all who have not received it.

76 But, verily I say unto all those to whom the kingdom has been given—from you it must be preached unto them, that they shall repent of their former evil works; for they are to be upbraided for their evil hearts of unbelief, and your brethren in Zion for their rebellion against you at the time I sent you.

77 And again I say unto you, my friends, for from henceforth I shall call you friends, it is expedient that I give unto you this commandment, that ye become even as my friends in days when I was with them, traveling to preach the gospel in my power;

78 For I suffered them not to have purse or scrip, neither two coats.

79 Behold, I send you out to prove the world, and the laborer is worthy of his hire.

80 And any man that shall go and preach this gospel of the kingdom, and fail not to continue faithful in all things, shall not be weary in mind, neither darkened, neither in body, limb, nor joint; and a hair of his head shall not fall to the ground unnoticed. And they shall not go hungry, neither athirst.

81 Therefore, take ye no thought for the morrow, for what ye shall eat, or what ye shall drink, or wherewithal ye shall be clothed.

82 For, consider the lilies of the field, how they grow, they toil not, neither do they spin; and the kingdoms of the world, in all their glory, are not arrayed like one of these.

83 For your Father, who is in heaven, knoweth that you have need of all these things.

84 Therefore, let the morrow take thought for the things of itself.

85 Neither take ye thought beforehand what ye shall say; but treasure up in your minds continually the words of life, and it shall be given you in the very hour that portion that shall be meted unto every man.

86 Therefore, let no man among you, for this commandment is unto all the faithful who are called of God in the church unto the ministry, from this hour take purse or scrip, that goeth forth to proclaim this gospel of the kingdom.

87 Behold, I send you out to reprove the world of all their unrighteous deeds, and to teach them of a judgment which is to come.

88 And whoso receiveth you, there I will be also, for I will go before your face. I will be on your right hand and on your left, and my Spirit shall be in your hearts, and mine angels round about you, to bear you up.

89 Whoso receiveth you receiveth me; and the same will feed you, and clothe you, and give you money.

90 And he who feeds you, or clothes you, or gives you money, shall in nowise lose his reward.

91 And he that doeth not these things is not my disciple; by this you may know my disciples.

92 He that receiveth you not, go away from him alone by yourselves, and cleanse your feet even with water, pure water, whether in heat or in cold, and bear testimony of it unto your Father which is in heaven, and return not again unto that man.

93 And in whatsoever village or city ye enter, do likewise.

94 Nevertheless, search diligently and spare not; and wo unto that house, or that village or city that rejecteth you, or your words, or your testimony concerning me.

95 Wo, I say again, unto that house, or that village or city that rejecteth you, or your words, or your testimony of me;

96 For I, the Almighty, have laid my hands upon the nations, to scourge them for their wickedness.

97 And plagues shall go forth, and they shall not be taken from the earth until I have completed my work, which shall be cut short in righteousness—

98 Until all shall know me, who remain, even from the least unto the greatest, and shall be filled with the knowledge of the Lord, and shall see eye to eye, and shall lift up their voice, and with the voice together sing this new song, saying:

99 The Lord hath brought again Zion; The Lord hath redeemed his people, Israel, According to the election of grace, Which was brought to pass by the faith And covenant of their fathers.

100 The Lord hath redeemed his people; And Satan is bound and time is no longer.

The Lord hath gathered all things in one. The Lord hath brought down Zion from above. The Lord hath brought up Zion from beneath.

101 The earth hath travailed and brought forth her strength; And truth is established in her bowels;

And the heavens have smiled upon her; And she is clothed with the glory of her God; For he stands in the midst of his people.

102 Glory, and honor, and power, and might, Be ascribed to our God; for he is full of mercy,

Justice, grace and truth, and peace, Forever and ever, Amen.

103 And again, verily, verily, I say unto you, it is expedient that every man who goes forth to proclaim mine everlasting gospel, that inasmuch as they have families, and receive money by gift, that they should send it unto them or make use of it for their benefit, as the Lord shall direct them, for thus it seemeth me good.

104 And let all those who have not families, who receive money, send it up unto the bishop in Zion, or unto the bishop in Ohio, that it may be consecrated for the bringing forth of the revelations and the printing thereof, and for establishing Zion.

105 And if any man shall give unto any of you a coat, or a suit, take the old and cast it unto the poor, and go on your way rejoicing.

106 And if any man among you be strong in the Spirit, let him take with him him that is weak, that he may be edified in all meekness, that he may become strong also.

107 Therefore, take with you those who are ordained unto the lesser priesthood, and send them before you to make appointments, and to prepare the way, and to fill appointments that you yourselves are not able to fill.

108 Behold, this is the way that mine apostles, in ancient days, built up my church unto me.

109 Therefore, let every man stand in his own office, and labor in his own calling; and let not the head say unto the feet it hath no need of the feet; for without the feet how shall the body be able to stand?

110 Also the body hath need of every member, that all may be edified together, that the system may be kept perfect.

111 And behold, the high priests should travel, and also the elders, and also the lesser priests; but the deacons and teachers should be appointed to watch over the church, to be standing ministers unto the church.

---

117 And verily I say unto you, the rest of my servants, go ye forth as your circumstances shall permit, in your several callings, unto the great and notable cities and villages, reproving the world in righteousness of all their unrighteous and ungodly deeds, setting forth clearly and understandingly the desolation of abomination in the last days.

118 For, with you saith the Lord Almighty, I will rend their kingdoms; I will not only shake the earth, but the starry heavens shall tremble.

119 For I, the Lord, have put forth my hand to exert the powers of heaven; ye cannot see it now, yet a little while and ye shall see it, and know that I am, and that I will come and reign with my people.

120 I am Alpha and Omega, the beginning and the end. Amen.

Duties and Blessings of the Priesthood: *Basic Manual for Priesthood Holders, Part B – The Father as Patriarch*

"Each family in the Church is a kingdom or government within itself. The father is the head of that government; he is the highest authority in the home and presides over all family functions. Concerning this matter, President Joseph F. Smith wrote: "It sometimes happens that the elders are called in to administer to the members of a family. Among these elders there may be presidents of stakes, apostles, or even members of the first presidency of the Church. It is not proper under these circumstances for the father to stand back and expect the elders to direct the administration of this important ordinance. The father is there. It is his right and it is his duty to preside. He should select the one who is to administer the oil, and the one who is to be mouth in prayer, and he should ... direct the administration of that blessing of the gospel in his home."

CONGRATULATIONS, YOUR SON IS A MAN!

MANCAMP ITEMS LIST
Holy Scriptures
Hatchet the Novel
(ISBN 0-02-770130-1)
Geocaching App for Smartphone Geocaching.com
Tin/Copper Sheets 5"x7" bound
Compass
Survival Bracelet(s)
Small Folding Pocket Knife
Rabbit Trap*
Slingshot
Deer Trap*
BB Gun (Red Rider)
Small Hatchet
Survival Knife (Bear Grylls)
Basic Bow and Arrows
A .22 caliber Rifle**
A 12-gauge Shot Gun**
A .30-06 .223 or .270 Rifle**
ManCamp Journal (Leather Bound)

*Item can be made in nature, or purchased from my website.
**Items are not available from my website directly, but I have links to direct you to a few firearms dealers.

A complete ManCamp kit (less-firearms), individual items, as well as a number of video tutorials (traps) are available from my website:
Also see my other publications, FamilyCamp, and GirlsCamp – Raising Girls into Women. Each offer a unique perspective on how to better communicate with your loved ones.

www.raisingboysintomen.com

"Fatherhood is not a matter of station or wealth, it is a matter of desire, diligence, and determination to see one's family exalted in the celestial kingdom. If that prize is lost, nothing else really matters." — President Ezra Taft Benson.

"The father is there. It is his right and it is his duty to preside. He should select the one who is to administer the oil, and the one who is to be mouth in prayer, and he should … direct the administration of that blessing of the gospel in his home."
-Duties and Blessings of the Priesthood

"May the Lord's choicest blessings rest upon all who seek to be a great Father."
-David G. Hamilton

ISBN 978-0-9887694-0-3

9 780988 769403 >

US $14.99 CND $15.99

www.ingramcontent.com/pod-product-compliance
Lightning Source LLC
Chambersburg PA
CBHW041404090426
42744CB00001B/1